Advance Prais

Most of us pray—and most of us don't feel we're especially good at it. What we need is an honest and experienced guide, someone who's shared our struggles and learned how to face them—and learned how to draw closer to God even through them. Alice Teisan is the ideal guide, and I'm delighted she shares her wisdom with us in this book.

—Kevin Miller
Senior Pastor, Church of the Savior, Wheaton, Illinois
Former Executive Vice President, Christianity Today

Against the gritty backdrop of a chronic and debilitating disease, Alice Teisan shows a way forward in the life of prayer. With a penchant for personal honesty and winsome transparency, she has provided us with a written mentor in Pray 10K. Grounded in her own experience and experiments with prayer, Alice's engaging illustrations and practical suggestions invite us to be similarly creative in reaching out to God. Judicious, meaty, and prodding quotations throughout the book evidence her deep engagement with the literature of prayer. With characteristic humility, the singular accomplishments of her life—including the founding of His Wheels International—are related simply as the fruit of prayer. Finally, Alice's willingness to share the intimate hurts and joys of journeying in prayer inspires us to exercise and strengthen our prayer muscles as well. I heartily recommend Pray 10K.

—Evvy Hay Campbell, Ph.D.
Associate Professor of Intercultural Studies Emerita, Wheaton College

Alice Teisan's new book, entitled Pray 10K, documents the prayer experience of a gifted person challenged by a chronic debilitating illness. Unlike a typical how-to treatise that features shallow platitudes or easy formulas for prayer, Pray 10K shares prayer patterns and struggles embodied in life experiences that speak louder than hollow pontifications. Everyday miracles of mundane health challenges and daily stresses are all bathed in prayer to enable feeble steps somehow, if not always triumphantly. The compelling prose of Alice's new book blesses the reader while it teaches important and practical lessons embodied in the practices of a person committed to vital prayer communion with the Savior. Better than reading a story, Alice's book allows the reader to study the prayer discipline needed for spiritual survival as expressed in the realities of one person's daily life.

—Terry Perciante, Ph.D.
Professor of Mathematics Emeriti, Wheaton College

This is a refreshing new book on prayer, written with the simplicity of a practitioner whose heart pants for streams of living water. It acknowledges the beauty of prayer as fellowship with the Triune God—Father, Son, and Holy Spirit, rather than as a shopping list for God to fulfill. It embodies prayer as an attitude of willful surrender to the supremacy of God's will rather than as a manipulative tool at the disposal of the creature. It epitomizes prayer as a quest to know and become more like Jesus, rather than attempt to demonstrate a spiritual superiority. In case you are wondering "why another book on prayer?" my answer is simple, why not? If I ever have the privilege of recommending a book on prayer to anyone, it would be a book written by an author whom I know very well as a lover of Jesus, one who practices what she preaches, one who has embarked on the pleasurable journey of enjoying the walk with Jesus as the means of working for him. In your hands is that book!

—Rev. Zachariah Chinne
Former Secretary, ECWA Bukuru District Church Council, Jos, Nigeria

No one needs another dictionary definition, another tidy oversimplification. That's not how you set out on the messy journey to authentic prayer and relationship with God.

So, in this book there are none of those head-on attempts to define the undefinable, to pin down God's behavior and reduce grace to a formula. Neither is this a plunge into mysticism nor an unreachable example of a perfect path. What you have in your hands is a sidelong approach to the question of prayer. The author tells a story—a gritty, deeply personal story. She shares the questions she has asked, the pain and disappointments she has endured, and the ways her life and work have been changed around her.

As she unfolds her life story, you too are invited to ask your own questions, to explore your own pains and triumphs, and to find the ways God is already reaching out for you.

Prayer is the focus of this book, but you will go away with more than just a "how to" for your personal devotions. This is also an account of how the author's dynamic His Wheels ministry emerged and evolved through those times of prayer—in the midst of struggles and unexpected moments of grace in her life as a regular, imperfect person. So, no matter how you will come to define the "ministry" of your own life, you'll come to feel how prayer, how God's companionship and transformative presence in your life, can grow your ministry into something that reaches outward to touch others all around you.

—Rachel Lambert, Millennial
Coordinator of volunteer stewardship at a not-for-profit native seed farm

My acquaintance with Alice began when a bicycling student group from Taylor University in Upland, Indiana, in 1988, allowed a very middle-aged secular Jew to accompany them on a bicycle tour in Israel. Among the other riders was a young nurse and very powerful bicycle rider named Alice Teisan who had already bicycled coast-to-coast twice. Alice was a few years older (26) than the other students and had much more experience with the outside world than they did.

I always found it enlightening to talk with her and especially to listen. That hasn't changed over the years, and it is one of the reasons, however strange it sounds, that as a Jewish atheist I am a founding board member of HWI.

This book is devoted to prayer, a subject on which Alice knows far more than I do. I think you will find that that puts you in her debt, and you will be glad to be there. To find out exactly what that statement means, read the book.

—Harvey Lyon, Ph.D.
A self-proclaimed Jewish atheist and a founding board member for His Wheels International

PRAY 10K

*How the Radical
Can Become Real*

Alice Teisan

Pray 10K How the Radical Can Become Real: A 10,000-Hour Prayer Adventure

Published by Alice Teisan, Wheaton, Illinois 60187.

Back cover photo of Alice Teisan thanks to Anette Ejsing

Cover designed by Gabriel De La Cruz

Library of Congress Cataloging-in-Publication Data: 2017903992
ISBN-13: 978-0-9882735-2-8 ISBN-10: 0-9882735-2-7

To those who call me
aunt, friend, coach, and mentor

Content

Introduction

Prayer Travelogue

The journey of a thousand miles begins with a single step.
—Lao Tzu

PRAYER IS A FASCINATING worldwide communication phenomenon. It encompasses cultural rituals of lighting candles and meditation, religious practices of gathering daily for prayer at set times, cries for help in a crisis, or even natural outbursts such as "OMG!"

Each reader will have his or her own prayer perspective based on culture, family, education, and life experiences. But one thing remains a constant: we all long for a satisfying connection with a person or power higher than ourselves.

An individual may wonder, *What am I missing?* Some might say, "I tried to pray, but God disappointed me—I'm not sure I'm ready to trust him again," or "God may answer your prayers, but he doesn't answer mine!" And most of us are baffled by the paradoxes of prayer that defy comprehension: it is rewarding yet frustrating, comforting yet disturbing, intimate yet foreign, and peaceful yet a battlefield.

What gives me the audacity to write on this topic? Over time, I have come to realize that there is a hunger for dialogue around prayer. There is also a Bible promise that states, "You will seek the LORD your God, and you will find Him if you search for Him with all your heart and all your soul."[1]

Through the pages of this book, I invite you to join in on my Pray 10K. This is a 10,000-hour travelogue in which I describe the route I took, the challenges I faced, the prayer fatigue wall I hit, the suffering I experienced, the vistas I explored, and the mysteries I discovered. I do not present this as a theological stance on prayer, but as a glimpse of how the radical became real. The only way to see, hear, know, or experience "the hidden truth (the mystic secret) of godliness,"[2] where God unveils *and* reveals true wisdom by his Spirit,[3] is through fellowship and communion with the Lord. This is prayer.

I hope Pray 10K will encourage you to take the first step that will lead to other steps in your own prayer journey. I trust that you, too, will experience what Joseph Seiss pens: "In the earthly we are to see the heavenly. From the typical we are to rise to the contemplation of the real."[4]

Personal Prayer: Loving Father in heaven, as I embark on this exciting journey, show me how to pray. I thank you for the promise that when I seek the Lord my God, I will find him if I search for him with all my heart (Deuteronomy 4:29). I commit each step of this journey to you, Father, in the precious name of Jesus. Amen.

QUESTIONS:
1. What are some of the prayer challenges you face?

2. What questions or comments do you have about prayer?
3. What prompted you to read this book on prayer?

1

Discovering the Need for Prayer

*If we lose our God, we lose our friends, who cannot help us unless God
be for us.*
—Matthew Henry

*L*ORD, *I'M NOT SURE if I still want to live for you! Does faith offer
any hope at all? If so, where can I find it?*

On New Year's Day, 1988, at the age of twenty-six, I boarded a
plane in pursuit of fulfilling an eleven-year childhood dream—riding
my bicycle through Israel with Wandering Wheels, a Christian cycling
organization. Before then, my academic calendar and the trip's
schedule never coincided.

I grew up in a Christian home, and the Christian culture and
lifestyle were part of my identity. At the age of twelve, I accepted
Jesus Christ as my Savior, following the instructions in Scripture: "If
we confess our sins, He is faithful and righteous to forgive us our
sins and to cleanse us from all unrighteousness."[5] The Bible goes on

to explain, "For there is one God, and one mediator also between God and men, the man Christ Jesus."[6] This was the first step on my spiritual journey, and it can be yours too. Now I could connect to God through Jesus Christ, my prayer mediator.

Over the next fourteen years I pursued what I perceived was a good Christian life, but I still felt depressed and troubled. By then I was a professional church-server, which I thought was synonymous with being a faithful Christian. I had been a Sunday school superintendent at a small church for three years, teaching classes, writing curriculum, coordinating in-services, securing substitutes when needed, and leading recreation for summer Bible school. My avocation infringed upon my full-time nursing vocation. Instead of living "the good Christian life," what I really did was serve myself into an emotional charbroiled, burnt-out spiritual state.

Just six months earlier I had declared, *God, I don't know if you are worth living for anymore!*, precipitating a war zone within my soul. I wasn't sure who would win the throne of my life or how I'd know when my crisis of faith had ended. I was desperate for hope and doubted whether trusting in God held the answers to my longings. But if not faith, then what were my options?

It was no coincidence that this was God's perfect timing for me to fulfill my dream of cycling throughout Israel. The bicycle trip was a January Bible college credit class offered by Taylor University (TU), with Wandering Wheels as the bicycle support. The team consisted of about forty people, most of whom were TU undergraduate students, professing protestant evangelical Christians, taking the class for credit. In addition, there were two professors, several Wandering Wheels staff members, and a few who were auditing the class, including myself. Two other auditors were Harvey, a traditional "Jewish atheist" by his own assertion, and a young Mormon gal, on mission to make me one of her converts.

We spent the initial four days exploring Jerusalem by foot with a local tour guide. Our first stop was at the Western Wall, known as the Wailing Wall before the Six Day War in 1967. "For centuries, especially on the 9th of Av, the anniversary of the Temple's destruction, the Jews would flock to the wall to moan their treasured loss."[7]

It was fascinating to encounter people of all spiritual backgrounds, a prayer rendezvous at a specific time and place each day, segregated into two sections—men and women. What a foreign concept to me. Then, hearing the vulnerable and varied emotional expressions gave meaning to its name—Wailing Wall. Prayers scribbled on little pieces of paper were shoved in the holes and crevices of the stone surface.

This left me with more questions and a need to research what the history was behind this prayer practice.

The next stop, the Via Dolorosa, took the concept of prayer to a deeper place in my heart. I couldn't push the words to Sandi Patty's song out of my head:

"Down the Via Dolorosa called the way of suffering
Like a lamb . . . He chose to walk that road . . . for you and
me . . . to Calvary."[8]

While meandering along the Via Dolorosa, I found myself unnerved while I continued battling, "Will I continue walking with Christ or reject him forever? How could he walk the road, loving me so much that he continued to Calvary to die for my sins, while I was trying to ditch him along the same route?" Sandi Patty's song just continued looping in my head.

A somber mood prevailed. Walking toward the Garden of Gethsemane, knowing this was where Judas betrayed Christ, only intensified my emotions. The same spot where he confronted his disciples about praying with him for one hour!

Gethsemane, the place of Christ's suffering, overwhelmed us with the price he paid for our salvation and ushered our group into a reverent silence, a hush. It seemed as though nothing could disrupt our worship-filled awe. Wrong! Seconds later, vying for our attention was an entrepreneurial Arab dressed up in his Middle Eastern garb and advertising camel rides, somehow knowing it was on every American tourist's itinerary. And judging by our team's response, he was right.

After the camels' dust settled, I remembered Jesus' words to Peter: "'Sit here while I pray. . . . My soul is very sorrowful, even to death. Remain here and watch.' And going a little farther, [Jesus] fell on the ground and prayed. . . . And he came and found them sleeping, and he said to Peter, 'Simon, are you asleep? Could you not watch one hour?'"[9] *How could I look down on Peter, after caving to the camel ride?*

The reverent and ridiculous scenario at the Garden was a visual reminder of the spiritual battle present around prayer. I would soon discover that the enemy constantly prowls around, ready to divert our attention. Tiny distractions always rush in while I'm attempting to quiet my heart. Thoughts like, *Oh, Alice, you forgot to do X, Y, Z.* Or, *You must pay bills 1, 2, 3 immediately. No, wait; aren't they automatically withdrawn from my checking account each month?* I wish the Garden of Gethsemane scene were a one-time episode. But it was not!

Why am I so easily distracted in prayer? I have discovered that since prayer is the heartbeat of our Christian life, Satan works overtime to thwart our prayer efforts. If the enemy can foil us from the reverence of prayer and cause us to run to the foolish, he has defeated us from effective Spirit-filled service to our Lord.

While continuing on to the next stop, the loudspeakers on top of the minarets around Jerusalem piqued my curiosity. They were especially prevalent in the Muslim Quarter of the Old City. It shocked me the first time I heard a person with a quality voice call the Muslim men to prayer. What a baffling sight through my Christian lens to watch them gather together, placing their prayer rugs down—when secret prayer was my spiritual and cultural norm.

On the fifth day, before leaving Jerusalem, our Wandering Wheels leader presented a short but memorable group devotional, reading Psalm 121:1-2: "I lift up my eyes to the hills. From where does my help come? My help comes from the LORD, who made heaven and earth."[10] He ended with a challenge: "As you look out over the Judean Hills on the horizon, that's where we will be bicycling today. While climbing uphill, fight the inclination from exhaustion to look at the ground. Instead, take time to look up and remember where your help comes from."[11]

Moments after beginning, with my bicycle pannier luggage loading me down, I could feel the ever-increasing resistance with each pedal rotation over the fifty-mile uphill climb. I'm not sure which challenge was stronger—the physical or the spiritual. I wondered if the invitation to look up would help me find God.

What I didn't discover until 2016 was how the Psalm 121:1-2 devotional given on my Israel 1988 trip became the road map for my spiritual journey. Alexander Maclaren says of these verses, "There are three things here—the look of longing, the question of weakness, the assurance of faith 'I will lift up mine eyes unto the hills'—a resolution, and a resolution born of intense longing."[12] Indeed, I went to Israel with such a longing. Cycling up the hills and looking to the heavens required what Maclaren goes on to write: "You will not do it unless you make a dead lift of effort. It is a great deal easier for a man to look at what is at his feet than to crane his neck gazing at the stars."[13] John Gill writes, "The lifting up of the eyes is a prayer-gesture . . . and is expressive of boldness and confidence in prayer."[14]

Then the question about help articulates our weakness. Maclaren's words are powerful: "Brethren! If, on the one hand, we have to cultivate, for a healthy, vital Christianity, a vision of the mountains of God, on the other hand we have to try to deepen in ourselves the wholesome sense of our own impotence, and the conviction that the dangers on the road are far too great for us to deal with. . . . Unless we, when we set ourselves to this warfare, feel the formidableness of the enemy and recognize the weakness of our own arms, there is nothing but defeat for us."[15]

In 1988, I longed for the assurance of faith, to know that the Lord was my help. Maclaren writes, "The assurance of faith follows the consciousness of weakness, and both together will lead, and nothing else will lead, to the realization of the vision of faith, and bring us at last, weak as we are, to the hills where the weary and footsore flock 'shall lie down in a good fold, and on fat pasture shall they feed upon the mountains of Israel.'"[16]

I don't know what I expected would happen while in Israel. The Lord certainly used the morning devotional from Psalm 121:1-2 as a spiritual arrow to pierce my heart. Those twenty-five words encompassed the three-part process required for a spiritually vibrant life. Moreover, I couldn't escape the Lord's pursuit.

The international emphasis on prayer and commitment bombarded my senses at the Wailing Wall, on the Vía Dolorosa, in the Garden of Gethsemane, through the Muslim prayer custom, and in contemplating David's words while ascending northward out of Jerusalem. It opened my eyes, broadened my horizons, and created a craving within my soul. At age twenty-six, my spiritual life was at a crossroads, a critical juncture. Living a complacent Christian life wasn't an option, but I was clueless as to what I was pursuing.

After five days in Israel I wasn't ready to end my faith war and recommit my heart to Christ. Nevertheless, the Holy Spirit was convicting me, and prayer kept haunting me.

Personal Prayer: Most High God, I am thankful for David's words. Teach me to lift up my eyes to the hills and onward to heaven for help. Cultivate in me a maturing trust and confidence that "my help comes from the LORD, the maker of heaven and earth" (Psalm 121:1-2). Forgive me, Lord, for the times I look sideways, downward, and every which way but upward to you for help. I confess my weakness is to gaze toward my bank account, trusting in money before you. Thank you for being patient with me, a sinner in need of the blood of the Lamb. In Jesus' name, amen!

QUESTIONS:

1. What are the unwritten rules in your mind of being a "good Christian?"
2. Where are you looking for help—upward or elsewhere?
3. Have you ever experienced a crisis of faith? If so, what was it? How did you resolve it? Or are you still struggling?
4. What tends to distract you during your prayer time . . . or distracts you from even getting started?

2

Trying to Pray for an Hour

Pray inwardly, even if you do not enjoy it. It does good though you feel nothing, even though you think you are doing nothing.
—Julian of Norwich

BY THE FIFTH DAY in Israel, my hardened heart was becoming as pliable as clay. Truth was penetrating my soul as the biblical sites and historical teachings were bringing spiritual clarity.

Now I had to consider the cost of being a disciple. *Was I willing to turn my life over to Christ?* I couldn't maintain a lukewarm Christian existence. I had to either unabashedly forge ahead for Christ or renounce him unwaveringly. My bone-dry "Christianity" wasn't an acceptable alternative any longer. Throughout my trip and afterward, I was disturbed by the question Jesus asked his disciples in the Garden of Gethsemane, "Couldn't you watch with me even one hour?"[17] Unsettled, I wondered, *How would this idea of praying one hour a day fit into my Christian life?*

13

Midway through our twenty-four-day trip, I received another spiritual jolt through a teammate. While I was riding alongside a hurting cyclist, encouraging her along, Harvey passed us and said, "Alice, I just have to say, you live your faith." Harvey, who refers to himself as a Jewish atheist, had no idea how his compliment wracked my last spiritual nerve. God's sovereign sense of humor captivated my attention.

Harvey's objective was to observe Israel through a Christian perspective. Of all the unlikely places for him to identify Christ, my life was one of them, where a war of allegiance was raging. Afterward, I pondered, *Was he on the trip to help remove the spiritual blinders that were hindering me from observing the Lord?*

Days later, I surrendered my life to Jesus, resolving the internal battle. Once we reached the Jordan River, I celebrated the rededication of my life to the Lord through a renewal of my baptismal testimony. As my head resurfaced, I declared, *I will follow you wherever you lead.*

The next memorable day was cycling away from the Dead Sea, the lowest place on earth at 1,312 feet below sea level. Off in the distance I spotted Masada, a desert fortress towering 1,476 feet above the Sea.

Arriving at Masada's base, it was apparent that there were two ways to make the ascent. The three-minute cable car ride grabbed my attention. No effort required, just a quick scenic aerial jaunt!

A dilemma remained—my bike! Hmmm—Snake Path was the alternate route! One book about the climb warns, "If you are a hearty soul (or think you are) [then you] climb Masada from the east." Such a climb can cause "an unusual strain on body muscles which have remained dormant since the last time you tried a fool thing like this."[18] Yikes! I hoisted my bike, setting the stabilizing bar on my shoulder before beginning the 1200-foot ascent up the two-mile-long Snake Path.

While climbing, I stared wistfully at the cable car. The effortless journey was my wish, especially when navigating the sharp twists and turns, feeling the pain of the protruding rocks penetrating my shoes to the soles of my feet. Traversing loose gravel, I feared losing my footing and tumbling backward. Having my bike fall on me would have been ugly! Midway up, winds gusted, followed by rain, leaving me exposed to the elements in the shorts and T-shirt I was wearing, since the follow-up van had transported our bike panniers that day. Upon reaching the peak, the drop in temperature chilled me to the bone. Meanwhile, a chill of a different kind walloped my spirit.

How could the same panoramic view that exhilarated me have left 960 Jews in the first century horrified and hopeless? I learned that the Jews on Masada were blindsided by the Roman army's advance, and all chose to commit suicide rather than succumb to their enemy. Choked with emotion, Harvey spoke the short Israeli oath of determination, which military cadets still make there. "Never forget. Never again." For me, Masada was holy ground, the spiritual fortress where I solidified the allegiance I had made in the Jordan River. *Alice, never forget God. Never again.*[19] I was comforted by a psalm, "The Lord is my rock and my fortress and my deliverer . . . in whom I take refuge."[20]

As the Israel trip ended, the prayer promptings whirled around my head. *How would prayer fit into my daily Christian life?* Puzzled, I wondered, *Are there two prayer roads—a cable-car and a snake-path version?*

"Can you not pray with me one hour?" Four months after returning from Israel, Pastor Lutzer of Moody Church in Chicago used that text for his sermon. While listening, I reminisced about a journal entry I'd jotted down in Israel. "I'd hate to have Jesus return and hear him say, 'Alice, could you not pray with me for one hour?'" That sermon was just for me.

When the service ended, I bolted home to launch into a new audacious prayer regimen, under which I would pray every day for one uninterrupted hour. With enthusiasm and trepidation, I knelt down at the side of my bed and plunged in. Having been a churchgoer for twenty-six years, since birth, I began, assuming it would be enjoyable. I had the same road map as the disciples. I could rattle off the "model prayer," also known as the Lord's Prayer, the

Paternoster, the Our Father, or the disciples' prayer guide. Wasn't Old English the reverent and formal way to pray, using the King James Version? Most of the senior saints I knew prayed using "thy" and "thou" instead of "your" and "you." If prayer was ongoing communication, building an intimate relationship between my heavenly Father and me, how did Old English and intimacy dovetail? I hadn't even begun, and I faced my first hurdle—what was the proper prayer English?

Next, I began reciting my itemized grocery-list requests. After filling my prayer shopping cart, my knees ached, my heart was restless, and only two minutes had passed. Devastated! A deluge of distractions flooded in and ousted the enjoyable prayer-hour fantasy. I struggled to concentrate, admitting, *I don't have any idea how to pray, how to connect with Divinity, or what that even means. Isn't prayer supposed to be a divine time, not a time of clock watching?* Befuddled, with fifty-eight minutes remaining, I mumbled, *How will I fulfill even the first hour of my newfound plan?*

Of course, somewhere during that hour I prayed the Lord's Prayer in the rote fashion I'd become familiar with during church services. Reciting the prayer was very different from comprehending the depths that Tertullian articulates: "In this prayer is comprised a compend of the whole gospel."[21]

What a disaster! After that first hour ended, I felt like a knee-knocking, prayer-fidgeting failure. I was ready to abandon my new intent. I had more questions about prayer than answers. How would I find a training program that would build my prayer muscle? Was my goal of one uninterrupted hour of prayer a day an impossible dream? What would I need to stay in the "prayer game"? Would I ever fulfill such a lofty ideal?

While evaluating that first hour, I acknowledged a need to adjust my expectations, knowing that I couldn't sustain a one-hour-a-day schedule. Since my interests and education revolved around health and athletics as a nurse and physical educator, I thought about solutions in terms of training schedules. Thus, I had to devise a successful spiritual training regimen that would build my prayer stamina over time.

One thing I understood from accomplishing several long-distance bicycle trips, including coast-to-coast twice (1977 and 1978), England and Scotland (1979), Israel (1988), and the Canadian Rockies (1990), was that training programs, at times, are excruciating. They require pushing the limits of all aspects of one's endurance. Then there is the other extreme of a conditioning fatigue, sometimes known as "hitting the wall." Performing something unique often produces discomfort, which requires balance to overcome the urge to quit or defer to something less demanding.

Throughout my prayer-training regimen I returned to the fundamental question: What is prayer? Answering the question required educating myself on the subject and agreeing with the disciples' first request to Jesus, "Lord, teach us to pray."[22] The Lord used as a tool the passages in Matthew 6:9-15 and Luke 11:2-4. But saying these prayers had become a rote speed-reading exercise, or a "prayer race," of sorts, so commonplace that it was hard to discover the meaning. I spent time studying these verses and prayerfully asking, "Lord, teach me to pray."[23]

Over the next two decades, while trying to grasp the scope of the Lord's Prayer, one exercise I tried was to formulate a who, what, when, where, why, or how question for each phrase. For example, "Our Father—who is he? Do I know his attributes, character, and Word? "In heaven"—what do I know about heaven? "Hallowed be your name"—how do I worship and honor the Lord? Only as I sought the Lord, as a student of prayer, did I begin to comprehend the perspective from which to pray, to change my problem-centered, fix-it method to a Kingdom focus. Afterward, I compiled a Concert of Prayer, incorporating these texts that I use as a prompt for intercessions on behalf of family, church, work, missions, government (local, state, national, and international), the world, etc.

As Broadman writes, "As such, this wonderful Prayer is suited to every age of the world and to every condition of life; equally appropriate for the little prattler bowing his head on his mother's knee and for the dying patriarch, for the closet and for the Ecumenical Council. And its petitions are as specific as they are comprehensive."[24]

In Appendix A, you will find The Concert of Prayer resource that is beneficial for individual, private prayer, or for group and corporate prayer settings.

Years later, while reviewing my initial uninterrupted prayer hour, I recognized the profound impact of that milestone. I didn't have warm fuzzy feelings, yet God was present and pleased by my prayers. Here are some important lessons I came away with from that first hour:

- It is hard work and an agonizing command, not a feeling.
- It is a time when all the distractions of life will descend.
- Time has a way of standing still.
- By showing up and resisting the opportunity to give up, I was engaging in spiritual battle and saying, "No, Satan, you will not win."
- Struggling to pray was the schoolroom where I continue to learn how to pray.

I was on a quest to cultivate my relationship with the Lord and to experience a vibrant faith. But if prayer was this daunting, I doubted it was the key that would unlock the door to an abundant spiritual adventure. Yet somehow, deep in my heart, I knew that without it I would not experience my full spiritual growth potential. From the outset, I grappled with "hitting the proverbial prayer wall." Although I was hoping for the painless Masada cable-car prayer path,

I realized that the route to my destination was via the snake path. After that first painful hour of prayer, I wondered, *What will I do now?*

Personal Prayer: Rock of Ages, you are "my fortress and my deliverer . . . in whom I take refuge" (Psalm 18:2). I confess that I run to you in need, but I often fail to make time for maturing my relationship with you, Lord Jesus. I am as guilty as your disciples were at the Garden of Gethsemane when you asked them, "Couldn't you watch with me even one hour?" (Matthew 26:40). Lord, forgive me for not prioritizing prayer time into my schedule. I'm ashamed to admit that I don't know how to pray. I cry out, pleading as your disciples did, "Lord, teach me to pray" (Luke 11:1). Amen.

QUESTIONS:

1. Are you considering an easy cable-car path? On the other hand, are you prepared to pursue the strenuous and grueling trails?

2. What prayer growing pains do you fear facing?

3

Trading Fantasy for Reality

Man is preoccupied with freedom yet laden with handicaps.
—Laura Hillenbrand

MY INITIAL HOUR OF prayer had left me pondering, *When and where did my interest in intense prayer begin?* Then I remembered my Colorado Rocky Mountain high adventure.

The year was 1984. After graduating from nursing school, I left my native Midwest residence in the rearview mirror as I floored the accelerator, my gaze fixed westward toward the snow-peaked Colorado mountains. I began my nursing career at a residential summer camp nestled in the foothills of the Rockies near Bailey, Colorado. I was on a quest for quietness and contentment and hoped it would just happen—like the aerial, cable-car Masada prayer ascent.

Dreams of relocating to Colorado had been six years in the making, originating in 1978 at the age of sixteen during my second coast-to-coast cycling trip with Wandering Wheels. Sixty-some riders traversed the Colorado Rockies, having begun in San Diego, cycling to Virginia Beach, covering 3,100 miles in six weeks.

The exhilarating, awe-inspiring beauty of the Colorado Rockies presented a spiritual magic for my rolling bicycle prayer altar. I was ushered into the majestic presence of my Creator, the Almighty God, for countless hours. The hymn "How Great Thou Art,"[25] summing up God's splendor, became my cycling prayer guide. With each pedal stroke, I admired the golden aspen trees and caught whiffs of the rich conifer scent rising from the forest floor. There, it was effortless to feel God.

The hymn continues: "Thy power throughout the universe displayed."[26] After climbing uphill for more than four hours in mid-July, with sweat dripping from everywhere, soaking my shorts and T-shirt, I crested the Continental Divide. While resting, before coasting down the other side, I felt the temperature shift as cold air barreled off the mountain peak. I then felt sleet, so in preparation for the decent I layered on more clothes.

God's power greeted me at every turn. The mountains inspired me to soar with the eagles, pant as the deer for water, and yearn for my Savior with a deeper intimacy. Unashamedly, I bellowed out, singing, "My Saviour God, to Thee, How great Thou art."[27] Yet somehow I was aware that my intimate, situational, mountain-high relationship with Jesus would trail behind as we continued east toward the monotony of the Kansas plains.

Never before had I felt God's presence so profoundly. I promised myself, *One day I will relocate to Colorado.* After traveling at a ten- to twelve-mile-an-hour pace for five days through mountain grandeur, I had formed a grandiose idea. Perchance, making the Rocky Mountains my permanent home, I would also inherit a continuous spiritual buzz. I was convinced the beauty was something that would never grow mundane, and that spiritual intimacy would only deepen.

After my seasonal summer camp position ended, I landed a position at a group home in Larkspur, twenty-two miles from Colorado Springs. There I would work with troubled teens who were one misguided step away from prison, in an alternative wilderness rehabilitation program. I could combine my interest in camping and my heart for youth with my professional nursing skills. The program included six months on-site, alternating with six months roughing it in the wilderness.

During the interview, the staff member asked, "What are your weaknesses in dealing with juvenile delinquents?" I articulated my concern, "I often get tangled up in power struggles with teens and lack the insight into how to diffuse them." The interviewer replied, "Don't worry. You will have a few weeks of training before being left in charge." Four days later, the welcoming words of my first day were, "Yesterday we cleaned house of the staff." Whatever that meant, it was unsettling, and the youth were spooked because the familiar was gone. No veteran staff remained, just a bunch of alien rookies like myself. There went the well-meaning interview affirmation, too. My position was half-time as a nurse, dealing with sexually transmitted disease issues; and the other half of my twelve-hour shift I spent as a "houseparent" for the same teen patients. The nurse/houseparent combination was another formula for disaster.

Three long, intense weeks later, my position abruptly ended with the words, "You're fired!" I don't remember the exact reason given, but it revolved around the weakness I stated up front—power struggles with juvenile delinquents. In addition, the inappropriate dual role of being a nurse and houseparent further escalated the rift in relating to the teens. Even though I knew the place was in chaos, a cloud of despair shrouded my soul. Less than six months after arriving in Colorado, encumbered with the shattered dreams of making my home there and holding the shambled pieces of my first permanent professional position, I headed back to the Midwest. "Shame-blame" baggage of being fired replaced the once mountain-high buzz.

Back in the Midwest, picking up the shattered pieces of my relocation dream while also trying to embrace the reality of my smarting heart, I wondered, *How will I ever find spiritual serenity in the familiarity of the Midwest?*

How would God ultimately use this disastrous scenario to give me a picture of my heart's longing? While aching for something I didn't have, I wondered, *Is "encountering God" some sort of evangelical gibberish?* What I would later learn is that the Lord was using those formative spiritual life experiences as prayer steps up the spiritual snake-path prayer ascent.

Fast-forward twenty years to a Bible study in 2004. The topic was intercessory prayer. Robert (Bob) Walker, the co-Bible study leader, gave an example that was God's gift to me. He explained that in the mid 1980s, Colorado Springs was overrun with witches who prayed, claiming the area for themselves and against Christians entering. Leaders of the National Association of Evangelicals (NAE) reclaimed the area for Christ through intense prayer. Bob went on to tell how New Life Church in Colorado Springs came out of these concentrated intercessory prayer sessions. Also in the years following, many Christian organizations were able to move their headquarters to Colorado Springs.

As Bob recounted the story, it resonated in my heart. It was a holy moment as I contemplated Larkspur, Colorado. *Maybe I've been asking the wrong questions all these years! Instead of what did I do wrong that led to my being fired, I should have been asking, heavenly Father what did you spare me from by having me leave Larkspur and move back to the Midwest? You have not been silent, nor have you been punishing me all these years for my failure. You, Abba Father, have answered my prayers—even back in 1984, when I was clueless about how to find you.*

By moving to Colorado, I was acknowledging my desire to experience Divinity. My illusion of a peace-filled sanctuary amid the pristine mountains evaporated, however, as I lived life. I had to admit that I idolized creation, but my heart longed to know how to worship the Creator.

It dawned on me that I could not replicate my early Rocky Mountain high worship experience by being in that same location. After all, it was the physical exertion of each agonizing pedal stroke forward that stimulated my sensory receptors, heightening my sensitivity to the awe of creation. It wasn't situational, but intentional concentration.

In retrospect, moving to Colorado was a way of testing my Rocky Mountain high theory. Now I understand that my magical hope for a thriving prayer life in the mountains was a crippling spiritual fantasy. I realized that if I were going to build an effective and comprehensive spiritual training program, I would need to first evaluate what had worked to this point and what had not.

Identifying spiritual Masada cable-car prayer fantasies along the way are vital to a prayer journey. Next, it is important to confess such illusions to the Lord. As we seek his guidance, he will keep us from being sidetracked while continuing our prayer ascent.

Personal Prayer: Father in heaven, I thank you for the privilege of entering your throne room through prayer. What a gift to be able to communicate with you anytime, anywhere, and about anything. Thank you for the hymn, "How Great Thou Art." Indeed, you are great and awesome. Discovering your wonders wherever we are is simply amazing. The splendor of your majesty is often closest to those who cry out to you from their sickbed or place of bondage. Thank you for a spiritual tenacity and stamina to devise and implement a training regimen that will build my prayer muscle, even when my feelings scream otherwise. Jesus, may my heart thirst for more of you each day. Amen.

QUESTIONS:

1. What promptings for prayer are swirling around in your mind?
2. What is a prayer story that has personally impacted your life in some way?
3. Recall an experience that indicated a spiritual desire in your soul.

4

Missteps along the Prayer Path

*The spirit of evil takes things that are right in themselves and perverts
them to our undoing.*
—G. C. Lorimer

A S I CONTINUED CONSIDERING the nature of prayer, I
asked, *What were some of the missteps along my formative prayer path?*

Recorded in my first prayer journal were a slew of teenage
struggles. "Lord, help me to stop putting a mask over my face, and to
stop playing a phony role as I seek for acceptance" (December 18,
1977). "Help me accept myself as one being molded into the person
you've meant me to be" (December 22, 1977). "I feel like a failure.
Help me realize I'm not" (July 29, 1980). "I wonder why I have the
abilities I have. Sometimes the pain digs so deep I just want to hang
life up. I wish I weren't human but supernatural. Lord, I want so
much to love others, but I just don't have it within me. I have such a

short temper span with people I love so much, like my mom, my dad, and my brother! Thanks for not being scared or intimidated by a frustrated child. Love, Alice" (1981).

According to Erickson's Developmental Stage Five—identity versus role confusion[28]—my teenage requests revolved around self-acceptance issues. These were age appropriate, but I didn't know it then. Clueless as to what constituted prayer, I longed for a role model with whom I could share the scribbled appeals hidden under lock and key. When my messy thoughts weren't met with immediate magical Masada cable-car-type answers, a form of prayer isolation, I became disheartened.

Looking back with twenty years of increasing maturity, I can now see my teenage cries were formational building blocks. Each was multifaceted, a Masada snake-path trek of sorts, which required making lifestyle choices, addressing self-acceptance issues, and dealing with emotional and psychological baggage. I can picture the Mighty Counselor's intricate answers in the form of a once empty prayer canvas now covered with countless brushstrokes of colorful details intricately placed by the Artist.

Without measurable markers, gauging our prayer efforts is arduous. Fear of erring in prayer can hinder us from authentically communicating with the Prince of Peace. I often wonder, *Is feeling spiritual intimacy during prayer a measuring stick for success? And should I interpret the opposite as failing miserably?*

As I thought of experiences, I recalled a high school situation that occurred when I was sixteen, in 1978.

Learning about a friend's serious accident, I visited him. When the elevator door opened onto the intensive care unit, an antiseptic odor accosted me, nurses in scrubs and doctors in lab coats scurried by, and I heard unusual sounds. Entering his cubicle, I saw tubes dangling from his comatose body and a machine forcing air into his lungs. While his chest rose and fell, my knees began wobbling. A queasy feeling struck as I broke out in profuse sweating. Spinning out of control, I thought, *Get me out of here before I drop!* Overcome with fear, unsure of what to do, a bargaining prayer escaped, *Lord if you save him, I'll marry him!*

What happened? Horrified, I gasped! *Was it a holy covenant I just prayed? Where did that crazy idea come from?* Propped up against a hallway wall in a fog, I fretted. *What am I supposed to do with all that has just barreled over me—the botched prayer that left me a prisoner along with the sensations, reactions, and questions that accompany the frailty of life?*

Guilt crushed me when the Great Physician restored my friend to full health. *Would the Lord judge or condemn me? Worse yet, if I didn't fulfill my part of the bargain, would I wreck my chances of ever getting married?* This crisis exposed an unvoiced prayer fallacy: God needed something from me before he would do his part! As if prayer involved negotiations of sorts!

Nevertheless, I feared sharing my predicament with anyone. Each time I saw or heard a verse that stressed the seriousness of keeping a covenant made with God, I cringed. For instance, "Be careful to perform what goes out from your lips, just as you have voluntarily vowed to the Lord your God, what you have promised."[29]

Prayer is an initial crisis response for many. Shock, a reactionary raw place of the heart, can leave us doing irrational, outlandish things, praying unguarded and senseless prayers, or blurting out absurd deals. Such a situation wasn't unique to me, but how was I supposed to know? I wish I'd found this quote from John Calvin years earlier, "God tolerates even our stammering, and pardons our ignorance whenever something inadvertently escapes us—as, indeed, without this mercy there would be no freedom to pray."[30]

The painful "crisis-bargaining-chip" prayer request scenario created havoc for another twelve years, until one day I blurted it out during a Christian counseling session. I uprooted a larger problem while unraveling this scenario. I had misinterpreted several scriptural passages into self-imposed torturous traps that created an "evangelical guilt trip" and stole my Christian joy. Even though I've never married, I know it isn't because God is punishing me for this prayer.

The Lord doesn't capitalize on crisis confusion. Samuel's encounter with God illustrates that if he wants to get our attention, he is patient and willing to repeat himself. He called Samuel three times. Each time Samuel went to Eli and said, "Here I am, for you called me."[31] Finally, Eli figured it out and instructed him on what to say in the future, but in the meantime told him to go back to bed! "Then the LORD came and stood and called as at other times, 'Samuel! Samuel!' And Samuel said, 'Speak, for Your servant is listening,'"[32] and the Lord spoke!

Another prayer situation that made an impression on me happened in 1981. Three weeks before heading off to nursing school, at age nineteen, I learned Brenda was in the hospital. *What's wrong with my good friend? She's only seventeen!* Brenda's mother told me, "On August 8, Brenda and I went to Eastland Shopping Mall. On our way home Brenda pulled her sleeve up and said 'Mom, look at this bruise on my arm.'" The bruise extended from Brenda's wrist to her elbow. Her mom said, "Brenda, we need to go to St. John's Hospital and find out what is going on." After examining her, the doctor came out to the waiting room and said, "I'm sorry to have to tell you this . . . she has leukemia!"

Detroit Medical Center was Brenda's next stop. A bone marrow transplant was the doctor's advice.

My friend's illness rocked my world. Dread segued into sadness, then anger, confusion, and the feeling of helplessness. *Now what?* I was in transition, caught up with the next chapter of my life—West Suburban Hospital School of Nursing in Oak Park, Illinois.

I owed Brenda a hospital visit! Her mother prompted me to go, but I procrastinated. Stymied by my own inadequacies, I told her and Brenda, "I am praying for your family." Prayer isolation was my spiritual cop out—my protective wall! How could I admit I was becoming intimidated, avoiding the dread of my first visit with a close friend battling a terminal illness? I didn't know then that I was running from grief and loss. *What will I say?* I wondered, *How am I supposed to act? What if I say something wrong? What if Brenda dies?* I mustered up the nerve to obey the dangerous Holy Spirit leading, and go. I took Brenda little gifts—balloons, stuffed animals, flowers, etc., but the real gift of presence was enough. Even thirty-two years later, her mom remembers that I took my guitar. She wrote, "You were such a blessing to her and to our family."

Once Brenda arrived home, she confided in me, "I really don't want to have a bone marrow transplant. But what do you think I should do?" I can still remember the harsh words I spoke under the guise of caring counsel. "Brenda, isn't it selfish for you not to undergo a transplant? Just think of your family and friends!"

In early September, as I left for nursing school, Brenda's family was heading off for Cleveland Children's Rainbow Hospital. With aspirations of finishing high school and one day becoming a lawyer still in her mind, Brenda realized how serious her condition was. As her family neared the hospital, she leaned over and said, "Mom, I may not come back home!"

They gave Brenda a 50 to 60 percent chance of surviving the leukemia, and with that, she underwent chemo and radiation, followed by a bone marrow transplant on October 23. Then on December 16, five days shy of her eighteenth birthday, Brenda died in her mother's arms, having never returned home. Her death caused me to admit, *God didn't answer my way!* While grieving, I teetered between replaying my lousy counsel and questioning whether prayer made any difference.

A few weeks later, in January of 1982 during my second semester of nursing school, I began a course on death and dying. I entered class thinking, "I could care less," attempting to disguise my heartache. The subject was our instructor Bev's areas of expertise. Not sharing my spiritual beliefs, Bev never substituted the stark reality of death with spiritually confusing sentiments like graduating, going home, passing on, or no more suffering. Her honesty, along with her gift of listening, allowed me to embrace the chaotic journey and quit faking happiness when feeling terrible inside. The course, over the next nine weeks, granted me permission to assimilate the grief process. With Bev at my side, I fumbled through trying to express my heart's cry. Admitting that death is charged with emotions and is never easy to process allowed me to stop kicking myself and to acknowledge that I had navigated Brenda's death as best I knew how. By determining to tread the grief trail, I gained some lifelong processing tools for myself and for sharing with others. A spiritual reality confronted me: the Mighty Counselor doesn't always answer prayer my way, nor is prayer a "super-natural" painkiller substitute, but an eternal-endurance enhancer!

As I moved on, I felt a skepticism of faith. I was accustomed to immediate rewards; thus, delayed gratification left me dissatisfied and wondering, *Is prayer just another "good Christian obligation?" I felt damned for my botched prayer efforts and damned when I didn't pray.* I knew the Bible "commanded" Christians to pray, but was this just another arbitrary "demand?" Pray or else!

Decades later, I found myself in a similar situation after learning that a church friend was in ICU on life support. The next morning while home praying with a heavy heart, I thought, *I should pick up my guitar and worship the Lord in song.* Then I sensed the Lord encouraging me to pack up my guitar and go pray, play, and worship at my friend's bedside.

It never gets easier to wrap my mind around the reality of the thief of death standing at the door of a life, yet this time I wasn't surprised by what I saw. Yes, the EKG was a perfect sinus rhythm (I could read it as a former cardiac rehab nurse), his chest was rising and falling consistently, there was brain activity, and the medical people were still able to draw blood. Yet I wondered if his body was here due to medical technology, while his spirit, as one who had committed his life to Christ, was already in heaven. As I played and sang worship songs in my friend's room, I watched many come in to see the devastating aftermath on his body with a terminal condition diagnosed only days earlier.

While praying silently, I played my guitar. I also prayed audibly with others. This time my prayers were different as I asked the Lord to comfort us in our grief. I gave thanks for our friend's life, filled with confidence, knowing that the Lord was in charge. I wasn't asking that my friend remain on earth in this state. The Lord knew he still had healing work to do through his life, for those who had to say their good-byes, for others needing hope that came from watching a church community rallying together, etc. True healing for each of us is when, as Christians who've bowed our knees to Jesus, we pass through the gates of death into heaven.

I wasn't practicing prayer isolation, allowing a prayer fantasy of healing to cause me to evade reality and prevent the grieving process. Instead, by granting myself permission to grieve, to cry, and to say good-bye, regardless of the outcome, I could also extend the same gift to his family and friends.

Yes, I was communing with the same Lord who raised Lazarus from the dead and could do it again if that were his plan.

Nevertheless, I wasn't in need of using prayer as a bargaining chip. Regardless of the outcome, I know God hears my prayers and he is still in control.

Gradually, I unearthed my misconceptions, reservations, and ineptness surrounding prayer. Indeed, there are times when communicating with the sovereign Lord reveals our stinky thinking or bad attitudes. When the Holy Spirit's spotlight shines on our sins, we must acknowledge and confess them to the resurrected Lord. As the psalm says, "May my prayer be counted as incense before You; the lifting up of my hands as the evening offering."[33] He delights in our prayers and invites us to approach him as children, not having everything figured out. Mistakes are part of growing in relational intimacy. Our Abba Father is perfect, patient and forgiving, full of mercy and grace, inviting us to come just as we are.

Personal Prayer: Abba Father, I come reverently into your presence. Thank you for Jesus, the mediator in prayer. Forgive me for wanting magical quick answers to prayer, void of trouble. Especially when considering how "Jesus was led up by the Spirit into the wilderness to be tempted by the devil and . . . fasted forty days and forty nights" (Matthew 4:1-2). I desire the attentiveness to your voice that Samuel displayed. When you call, may I obediently respond, "Speak, LORD, for your servant is listening" (1 Samuel 3:9). Then give me the courage to obey. In Jesus' name, amen!

QUESTIONS:

1.   What is your understanding of prayer?

2. From where did your ideas of prayer originate?
3. What expectations do you have about prayer?
4. Describe one of your prayer blunders.

5

Cultural Prayer Practices

When you pray, move your feet.
—an African proverb

WHEN CONSIDERING SOME OF the cultural highlights
from my Israel trip in 1988, I reflected on a variety of prayer
features that captured my attention. They included the regular
routines, daily rhythms, intricate patterns, and public expression.

For instance, at the Wailing Wall people from the four corners
of the earth streamed out of tour buses to lift their prayers silently,
conversationally, or artistically through song or drama to their god, or
to the Sovereign One.

This international scene with its varied religions and nationalities
sparked further questions. The visible communal rituals at the
Wailing Wall allured me, forcing me to ask, *Why is there such a tendency
in American evangelical culture to keep our prayers quiet?* Indeed, I know the
Scripture verse from where our fixation stems: "But when you pray,

go into your room and shut the door and pray to your Father who is in secret."[34] I suspect we've mishandled the secretive component of private prayer. The tendency in the American evangelical culture to keep prayer life private creates a fear of broaching the topic of personal prayer with another person, while we silently declare Satan the victor. It was a challenge to sift through my prayer confusion.

Only a short distance above the Wailing Wall, at the Dome of the Rock, sits El Aksa, the third holiest Muslim shrine.[35] Here is a visible case study about prayer, where the beauty is a magnanimous invitation to engage Allah. Upon entering, everyone must remove his or her shoes, a reminder of holy reverence. "The floors are covered with lush, priceless oriental rugs . . . 280 square feet built in the basilica fashion, assemblies of about 5,000 worshipers are possible, . . . on either side of the nave, up high on the walls, is a row of 21 windows made from Hebron stained glass."[36] And there are beautiful marble pillars throughout. Surrounded by fellow worshippers, immersed in beauty and reverence, Muslim men would kneel to Allah, saying prayers five times a day.

From the Dome of the Rock, I learned that a holy place of worship is one immersed in beauty, a place of soul receptivity. Such serenity is an invitation to enter into a Sabbath rest, captivating our hearts, orienting our minds, and renewing our souls. The warmth of color combined with sunlight provides a welcoming atmosphere to quiet our hearts and to lift our praises to the sovereign Lord. The Creator of the universe created humankind to engage, foster, and ponder beauty as part of worship. As a congregation provides space and sets aside time to seek the Lord in his temple, then within community we can bring to light and address the issues that need reshaping. Yet in the American evangelical church, we are in danger of becoming more concerned about comfort and friendly confines, appealing to the world by ditching tradition and hiding symbols of worship, than concerning ourselves with reverence, which facilitates transformation.

"Solomon's Temple was a beautiful place of worship and prayer. It was the center of Jewish religion, the place of God's special presence. However, a beautiful house of worship doesn't guarantee heartfelt worship of God. God wants to live in our hearts, not just meet us in a sanctuary."[37] Paul wrote, "Do you not know that your body is a temple of the Holy Spirit who is in you, whom you have from God, and that you are not your own? For you have been bought with a price: therefore glorify God in your body."[38] It causes me to pause and ask myself, *How am I adorning God's temple? Is my life shining with his beauty and glory? If so, how? If not, why not?*

The next stop on our tour was Gethsemane, where Christ had prayed three times to have the cup taken from him if it were the Father's will. God fulfilled his plan, but the road for Christ was that of suffering, not entitlement, as he drank the cup.

Christ's example at Gethsemane is a reminder of his attribute of love for us. In addition, his holy jealousy makes him intolerant of any counterfeit gods or idols sharing our soul's residence with the Lord. The ultimate purpose of prayer in a Christian's life is to glorify God in and through our life as we worship him alone. Prayer is not a tourist attraction, cable-car-like excursion where we "travel 900 meters in 3 minutes from the eastern side of Masada to the top of Masada."[39] Prayer is not the answer for finding a happy, healthy, or a wealthy life. It is the interaction of our soul with the light of Christ, where clarity shines into our chaos and confusion. As we persevere and agonize with Christ, as he did with the Father, we deepen our relationship with our Masada, our Mighty Fortress in the middle of a barren land.

The Apostle Paul described what I longed for in my relationship with Christ—"that I may know him and the power of his resurrection."[40] I knew that part of the verse and had bought into it, but the next phrase was more than I dared to pray—"and may share his sufferings, becoming like him in his death."[41] While moved with the scene of Christ's suffering at the Garden of Gethsemane, I grappled with the perseverance that would be required for traversing the complex twists and turns along my journey of prayer and intimately knowing God. What I didn't know then was that in 1992, at the age of thirty, suffering would become my intimate companion.

These international examples of prayer made an impression on me and sparked a question: *What were the American evangelical prayer traditions I grew up practicing?*

At home, prayer was often the "first course" of our evening family meal. A tradition passed on from my mom's childhood dinner table to ours went as follows: "Thank you, Lord, for Jesus Christ and for the blood he shed. For light and life and health and home and for our daily bread. Amen." There's nothing wrong with repeating written prayers, except when, as in my case, the repetitiveness became my "meal ticket," a verbal mealtime ritual void of heart.

Another prayer conundrum revolved around sharing a meal at home or at a restaurant with others. *What are my interior motives for praying before eating?* An internal dialogue raged. *Was I making a prayer scene, taking advantage of my captive audience and fulfilling my hidden agenda of witnessing to nonbelievers? On the other hand, was praying in a crowded restaurant a heart-formulated action consistent with what I did in my private life?*

Something else I remembered was the midweek church prayer meeting, an American evangelical tradition I participated in at a few different churches. There, a small number of attendees gathered. The services were structured much the same, beginning with a hymn followed by the pastor giving a thirty-minute Bible lesson. Afterward, there was an opportunity for those present to share praises and prayer requests. A litany of similar sounding physical ailment-type requests left no time for praises. That time was replaced with what seemed like eavesdropping on a stranger's private doctor-patient dialogue, intermixed with "unspoken requests." Such requests swallowed up every minute until the ending buzzer sounded. And we hadn't even started to pray yet—a common prayer meeting syndrome. Then one person was picked to cover all the requests in a quick parting way, dipping into overtime, as we scurried to leave on time.

I left those meetings frustrated by what appeared to be a prayer avoidance tactic, yet I returned week after week as the eternal optimist. *Everyone present knows how to tell time, right? Surely, next week we will make time to pray! Wasn't that what we'd come to do? Or was prayer really a Bible study, because we never ran out of time for that part of the meeting?* I couldn't muster any enthusiasm or stamina to pray again throughout the week for the long list of "medical diagnoses." I longed for something I didn't know I was missing—prayer teaching, training, and modeling.

The only other tradition I was vaguely familiar with was the Rosary—a set of beads hanging from car rearview mirrors as a tangible reminder for prayer. "Roman Catholics now think it very devout to repeat many times—often fifteen, and in some cases a hundred and fifty times—the Ave Maria (Hail, Mary), and the Pater Noster (Our Father, i.e., the Lord's Prayer), and count the repetitions by slipping the beads of the rosary—thus employing the very prayer our Saviour set, in contrast to such notions and practices." [42] Most Catholics are unaware of the history behind the Rosary. It was "a Buddhist practice, which came through the Mohammedans to the Spanish Christians." [43]

Alexander Maclaren says this about the Rosary beads: "And it is not without significance that this very prayer of our Lord's, which was given as the corrective of vain repetitions and idle, heathenish chattering of forms of prayer, has itself come to be the saddest instance in all Christendom of these very faults, while the beads slip through the fingers of the mechanical repeater of muttered Paternosters." [44]

As a young Christian, I was confused and wondered, *Why do the Catholics use beads when they pray, while my church doesn't use anything?* What I discovered as the years went by is that even though the Rosary is controversial, at least the Catholics have a prayer tool, something that is lacking in the evangelical practice.

Instead of having a prayer tool, I had a secretive falling-into-bed prayer ritual, a sleeping-pill-prayer habit. *Lord, I want to thank you for today! Give me a good night's . . . ZZzzzzzzz!* Jolted back to consciousness, I'd end again, . . . *um God, give me, a good night sleep, a— (snore) men.* I was lulled to sleep yet again by the most effective sleeping pill alternative—prayer!

Actively remembering the crowds gathered at these international prayer sites provided a catalyst for breaking free from my cultural prayer comfort zone.

Personal Prayer: "Our Father who is in heaven, hallowed be Your name. Your kingdom come. Your will be done, on earth as it is in heaven" (Matthew 6:9-10). I echo the words of your disciples, "Lord, teach us to pray" (Luke 11:1). I declare with Paul, I want to "know Him and the power of His resurrection and the fellowship of His sufferings, being conformed to His death; in order that I may attain to the resurrection from the dead" (Philippians 3:10-11). With a childlike faith, I ask, oblivious of what my request entails. Lord, patiently teach me to pray. Amen.

QUESTIONS:
1. Who taught you to pray or modeled prayer for you?
2. What prayer traditions do you remember from your childhood?

3. What alternative prayer traditions have you witnessed or experienced?

4. What did you glean for your personal prayer life from the prayer traditions of others, even those from Christian denominations different from your own?

5. What prayer traditions are not working for you? How can you improve or replace them?

6

A Path Less Traveled
Nontraditional Prayer Expressions

*Tears are the best prayers. No devout expressions, no liturgical
language, has such influence in heaven as tears. Tears are electric with
the best natures here: and are they not so with the Highest?*
—David Thomas

MY INITIAL PRAYER PREMISE was that God needed me to
carry the conversation. Dictating the orders, I expected the
Lord to fill them immediately as if I were the "Almighty Doctor"
calling my prescriptions in to the "pharmacist"—and no substitutes
accepted!

A prayer entry from February 1989 began

Dear God,

*I hurt like all get-out. I'm exhausted, sad, lonely, unhappy, disheartened,
discouraged, and disappointed . . . as I hold broken and shattered dreams and
hopes . . . I dread making this massive decision before me. It's too hard and too*

painful. I wish it could work out. Then I wouldn't have to have faith regarding your plans. Trusting you and your timing is out of my control and incredibly hard to do!

Writing out my prayers is one of the best ways for me to articulate my intimate thoughts by honestly spilling the ugliness of my heart onto paper. Prayer journaling helped me identify recurrent themes of anger, self-hatred, depression, etc. Yet I faced a dilemma! Guilt ridden, I wondered, *What's wrong with me? Am I the only one dealing with these or other such struggles? Moreover, how am I supposed to know?*

During corporate prayer meetings, I don't remember hearing those older than I modeling personal confessions or requesting prayer for intimate struggles or addictions. All too often, it seems like accepting Jesus is the beginning and ending of our conversion experience. However, Paul said, "But we all, with unveiled face, beholding as in a mirror the glory of the Lord, are being transformed into the same image from glory to glory, just as from the Lord, the Spirit."[45]

Paul also emphasized prayers of giving thanks and blessings in all of his epistles, versus a fix-it approach, which I didn't catch through modeling. For example, "Blessed be the God and Father of our Lord Jesus Christ, who has blessed us with every spiritual blessing in the heavenly places in Christ, just as He chose us in Him before the foundation of the world, that we would be holy and blameless before Him."[46]

My journal also helped me uncover reprimanding themes that kept reappearing. *If I only prayed longer, harder, more frequently, with more faith or was a "good enough pray-er," then these issues wouldn't have to see the light of day.*

With some prayers, I presented my urgent needs as a patient expecting to receive a "prayer-biotic broad-spectrum cure-all prescription" for healing my broken heart and allowing all my dreams to come true after a five-day request regimen. If the Lord had given his stamp of approval or licensure, it would have allowed me to continue my wrong view of prayer, thinking I could approach the

Lord as if I were the "Almighty Doctor" ordering the "pharmacist" around forever.

However, it didn't happen in my imagined way—by pushing the issues under the spiritual prayer carpet! God didn't send the answers through a speedy prayer-gimmick delivery system, which left me to my own assumption: *he doesn't have any intention of acknowledging or answering my prayers, does he?* My doubts continued while I tried silencing the relentless impulses to seek help from others in the body of Christ. It was unclear to me then that they were promptings from the Lord. On the other hand, maybe I was blissfully wishing he wouldn't make me take "these issues" on such a public road!

In my head, I knew his Word was true and that he cared about me. However, there was a long and unexplored chasm between my head knowledge and my heart knowing. While learning to trust and obey God's leading, one of his attributes—patience—helped bridge the intellectual-spiritual gap. "The Lord is not slow about His promise, as some count slowness, but is patient toward you."[47]

Even though I was seeing a Christian counselor by 1989, I finally confided in one of my prayer partners and asked for input. Her guidance terrified me: "I think you need to share even these issues with your counselor." Courageously, one hesitant step at a time, with my counselor's help and with my friend's encouragement, I embarked on God's dangerous adventure up the Masada snake-path of bona fide prayer. Through the process, I learned that prayer is not presumption upon God.

Identifying what weighs our spiritual life down and then becoming unshackled is an ongoing process fueled by the prayer elements of obedience, confession, forgiveness, and reconciliation. Demanding that somehow God owes me health and human comfort is not biblical. Only as I respond to my Master's instructional promptings can I keep the heavenly communication lines open.

The next section of that February 1989 journal entry consisted of an ink doodled smiley face, a cross overarching the whole picture, mountains off to the side (representing prayer), and a bicycle right in the center. Back then, I would have interpreted it as a scribbling distraction. I couldn't see past my personal confusion. Nevertheless, my doodling would one day represent a banner of hope, the glorious outcome of a comprehensive step-by-step spiritual growth process. The Holy Spirit's leading transcended my self-imposed thought that there was only one way to pray—with well-formulated coherent sentences.

In 2016, as I looked back on my February 1989 breathtaking prayer doodle, I burst out in triumphant glee. God had a plan for my life, a ministry that he would uncover in 2005. This picture personalized the following Scripture for me: "Likewise, the Spirit Himself helps us in our weakness. For we do not know what to pray for as we ought, but the Spirit intercedes for us with groanings too deep for words."[48]

As my understanding of prayer has matured, I have continually found new ways to bring the endless creativity within me before heaven's throne, adding richness to Holy Communion. In addition, I've learned that different prayer postures can assist when facing an ocean of emotions as we ride the waves of prayer.

How do I hold the Lord in my heart and communicate myself through prayer? This question invites me to explore the diverse ways to communicate with the Divine. Throughout the years, I have written a few simple worship songs that I've strummed on my guitar and belted out exuberantly. At other times, experiencing Handel's *Messiah* through the performances of The Choir of King's College, Cambridge, and The London Philharmonic has ushered me into the heavenly throne room.

Then there are times when I dream in silence and draw while prayerfully listening to Scripture. On other occasions, I have combined walking, drawing, and praying. During these exercises, I've been awed by the multiple splashes of color God uses to paint each sunset.

While attempting to draw a tree in nature, the grandeur and sovereignty of the Lord's artistic details dazzled me anew. Intricacies including light, shadows, perspective, depth, vision, angles, seasons, climate, color, patterns, etc., all originated with him. Through drawing, a new prayer venue for me, I am experiencing the words of Jean-Baptiste Camille Corot (1796-1875): "I pray every day that God make me like a child, that is to say that He will let me see nature in the unprejudiced way that a child sees it."[49] These discoveries are ways that prayer has revolutionized my reality. They impressed upon me that I'd always be an art student, continually learning new things from the Master Artist. John Calvin writes, "All the arts come from God and are to be respected as divine inventions."[50]

I've never attempted to draw portraits, but Van Gogh's words emphasize the depths of spiritual discovery that can be gleaned: "I'd rather paint people's eyes than cathedrals, for there's something in the eyes that isn't in the cathedral—although it's solemn and although it's impressive—to my mind the soul of a person . . . is more interesting."[51]

While contemplating creation, I remembered what a friend once told me: "Alice, what's unique about you is that when you pray, you believe God will answer." With the backdrop of what God has already done and continues to do, my requests are as child's play for the Almighty One.

On a grander and more sophisticated scale, isn't that what Christian artists like Paolo Veronese must have done when painting *The Wedding at Cana?* He painted it "in 1563 for the Benedictine Monastery of San Giorgio Maggiore in Venice. It depicts the first miracle Jesus performed when turning water into wine." Set in his time, "it is said that Veronese painted himself among the 130 participants of the wedding feast."[52] Here, art teaches and echoes the truth of prayerful contemplation of Scripture, portrayed with Christ at the center—a glorious, colorful interpretation.

In Veronese's later works, for example *Feast in the House of Levi*, 1573, which he first titled *The Last Supper*, he took artistic liberties too far. The Inquisition questioned him as to why he included "Germans, jesters, or buffoons in this picture. . . . Shouldn't painters only add figures in keeping with the subject and the most important people portrayed? Do you freely follow your imagination without restraint, without good judgment?"[53] Veronese replied, "My paintings are made with all the consideration I can bring to bear on them." The decree in the end was "that the artist must correct his painting within three months from the day of the reprimand, in accordance with the judgment of the Holy Tribunal."[54] He refused and instead renamed the picture.

Art is a helpful tool, but it can't be the only facet of our union with Christ. It can help release our imagination, opening our souls to fresh ideas in relating to him. But if art becomes too sophisticated, taken to an extreme, it can enslave us by creating idols we worship. Christian history has many examples of this dangerous extreme. Michelangelo writes the following in a sonnet (LXIV) about the voyage of life:

Now draws my life's long voyage to its close . . .

Which made of art my idol and my queen
I know how fraught with error it hath been . . .

Chisel nor brush shall satisfy again
The soul which to love divine doth turn,
That oped its arms to us on Calvary.[55]

Another historical guide is praying through the book of Psalms. Eugene Peterson writes, "For the last hundred years scholars have given careful attention to the particular form that the psalms take (form criticism) and have arranged them in two large categories, laments and thanksgivings. The categories correspond to the two large conditions in which we humans find ourselves, distress and well-being. Depending on circumstance and the state of our soul, we cry out in pain or burst forth with praise."[56] Peterson goes on to say, "Honesty is essential in prayer, but we are after more. We are after as much of life as possible—all of life if possible—brought to expression in answering God. That means learning a form of prayer adequate to the complexity of our lives."[57]

Back to my February 1989 journal entry, my prayer follows Peterson's points as found in the Psalms. There is lament in the first section, a hidden thanksgiving doodling in the middle, and a concluding paragraph with the cry of my heart: "Father, can you hear my silence, my sadness, my broken and my shattered dreams? I'm lost, hurt, lonely, and . . . "

Scripture says, "There is nothing new under the sun,"[58] including our struggles. Thus, I had to grapple with how I would embrace my chaos, sitting with it before the cross. Would I ever overcome the urge to run away from the pain and instead just accept, listen, and learn the lessons encompassed within? Gurnall, a writer from the 1600s, said, "There are so many professors and so few Christians indeed; so many that run and so few obtain; so many go into the field against Satan, and so few come out conquerors; because all have a desire to be happy, but few have courage and resolution to grapple with the difficulties that meet them in the way to their happiness."[59]

The ongoing journey of prayer provides repeated opportunities to grapple with the difficulties that present themselves. As we commune with the Lord, we must recognize that some of the hard work is facing battles in the heavenly realm. We shouldn't beat ourselves up when these intense struggles leave us fighting to remain on task and keep our thoughts present. Feelings are not a gauge for spiritual intimacy.

Just as an athlete sometimes hits the physical training wall, so too those running the spiritual race face the same training highs and lows. Workouts always challenge us to improve our skills, whether physical or spiritual. There is no such thing as a place of perfect praying. One of the spiritual perks is when we lose ourselves in God's leading, the outcome is often an unexpected heavenly starburst.

Prayer happens when a loving heavenly Father draws us as little children to the trailhead of the most amazing path, beginning with the perceived danger of sharing our intimate hurts, thoughts, and concerns. How much nearer to God would we be if we patterned our prayers after the prayers of children? Here are a couple of examples from Stuart Hample's book, *Children's Letters to God.* "In Sunday school they told us what you do. Who does it when you are on vacation? Jane . . . . Dear God, I read the Bible. What does begat mean? Nobody will tell me. Love, Alison."[60]

Matthew Henry says, "When there is communion between a soul and Christ, it is he that *begins the discourse*. He said unto them, *'What seek ye?'* It is a kind invitation of them into his acquaintance: 'Come what have you to say to me?' . . . The question Christ put to them is what we should all put to ourselves when we begin to follow Christ: *'What seek ye?* What do we design and desire? Do we seek a teacher, ruler and reconciler? In following Christ, do we seek the favour of God and eternal life?'"[61]

Here, a loving Lord accompanies us into an intimate healing process of self-examination that leads to healthy authenticity. Within this place, the Shepherd can uncover the sin that hinders us from "the freedom for which Christ has set us free."[62] It is a Divine invitation to remove the veil behind which we often hide. In the process, we are so overwhelmed by the unconditional love of our heavenly Father that we yearn to be made more into his image.

Prayer is the oil that lubes a chain of events on the road to a solution. It is a long-distance life endeavor, an aerobic exercise that requires continuous oxygenation from the Holy Spirit. Not a quick anaerobic burst of nonoxygenated fumes and then it is finished. As I read the first part of my prayer journal more than two decades later, I could see all of the ways God had faithfully answered. The Lord's best wasn't the road to freedom and joy I would have chosen.

Personal Prayer: Sovereign Lord, and Creator of my life, thank you that "the Spirit Himself intercedes for me with groanings too deep for words" (2 Peter 3:9). Thank you for your grace and patience along life's journey. Reveal the heart issues that weaken my spiritual authenticity. In Jesus' name, amen!

QUESTIONS:

1. What various forms of prayer have you tried (Psalm 150)?
2. What are some barriers to alternative expressions of prayer?
3. What will you commit to try as a new expression of prayer?
4. Whom might you entrust with this idea of prayer?

7

Dodging the Darts

There is no height the believer can attain where he is beyond the reach of Satan's darts . . . Even when 'made to sit together with Christ in heavenly places,'—when on the mount of transfiguration with our Lord, the darts of the wicked one may reach us, and plunge us in the ditch! O God, be not far from us when trouble is near: 'hold up our goings in thy paths, that our footsteps slip not!'
—William Garden Blaikie

THE OUTCOME OF BEING attuned to God's voice and then trusting and obeying his directions strengthens our ability to identify his sovereignty along with Satan's shrewdness in the midst of spiritual warfare. Recognizing that prayer isn't just one-dimensional—asking, at times begging, even demanding handouts on behalf of others and for myself—arms us for battle. Since I lacked any prayer discipleship in my formative years, I was often disillusioned when the Lord didn't answer instantly or in the way I presented it to him, leaving me vulnerable to Satan's taunts. I questioned, *Is prayer just a waste of time and energy, or does it really matter?*

Nevertheless, as Paul so eloquently wrote in Ephesians, prayer is multidimensional, "For our struggle is not against flesh and blood, but against the rulers, against the powers, against the world forces of this darkness, against the spiritual forces of wickedness in the heavenly places."[63]

I recalled a desperation-filled attempt at finding God in 1974. At the age of twelve, as a new Christian, intending to spend the day with God, I gathered my Bible, *Gill's Commentary* from the 1700s, and my *Strong's Concordance* and placed them on our round living room table. I plopped in a chair and hunkered down over my open Bible and commentary, as I began my spiritual quest of connecting with the Lord through study and prayer.

Time dragged on. The deceiver haunted me, and within twenty minutes I felt like "a total prayer failure at finding God." Unable to bear Satan's tantalizing a minute more, I abandoned the uncharted holy place to resume the familiar—kicking a football, swinging a tennis racket, and cranking on bicycle pedals.

Now as I reflect on that experience, what I lacked back then was the knowledge of Satan's schemes. John Calvin calls prayer, "the chief exercise of faith."[64] Knowing the importance of prayer, why wouldn't Satan hurl all the darts he could to thwart my prayer plans? By detonating my desire and instilling in me the lie "of being a prayer failure," Satan won the battle. The constant adrenaline charge from the hustle and bustle of the twenty-first century American culture had, by nature, conditioned every fiber of my being and driven my existence.

Recalling my nursing school days, the words from my class advisor, Michelle, often haunted me as they ricocheted in my brain, "Can't you ever sit still? Do you always have to be doing something?"

In the late '80s, if my hope for a weekly, uninterrupted hour of prayer was any indicator of my ability to sit still, the answer was a resounding, NO, I can't sit still! I am hyper-aware that society rushes on, and I fight the irrational fear of "missing out on some important opportunity." Everything from a marketer's phone call, to getting together with friends, to going to a ballgame seemed more urgent than prayer. Always doing something guaranteed I wouldn't encounter the most frightening foreigner prowling around—myself!

All the lines about wasting time blared in my head, creating a guilt-laden cloud when I bowed my head to pray. They seemed to echo society's messages about prayer: "Don't just sit there, do something! Quit wasting time!" "Hurry up; it's time to get going." On the other hand, "There's not much time left before we have to . . ." Everything in me urged, *Go and do. Don't stay and pray.*

Another obstacle to genuine prayer is the evangelical culture's "formula" etched on my heart from childhood that equates Christian service with Christian life. After sharing my emotional turmoil on multiple occasions with a variety of mature Christians, the concept was the same. If I just served more, then I wouldn't be so self-focused. Instead, I'd be helping others whose problems were guaranteed to be worse than mine. Longing to find the joy of the Lord, I gave myself fully to focusing outward, believing that service, an action-packed way of doing something for Christ, was the magical spiritual-emotional formula suggested during my teenage years. But it didn't happen!

I can't recall an emphasis placed on prayer in my teenage years. There were mentors for service, but not for prayer. It would have created quite a conflict back then if someone had told me to set aside chunks of time for prayer when I was experiencing depression and confusion. How could I have entered into such a holy contemplative place—bringing my brokenness, despair, helplessness, and pain to the Lord and being still in his presence? What a polar opposite to serving Christ and turning my focus outward. Believing the lie that, somehow, service is a solution for a troubled soul, productivity is a measure of importance, and time is money, had duped me. In retrospect, I can see that Michelle valued me enough to confront my unhealthy, obsessive, multitasking behavior.

One problem working against me was my inability to sit still. The bigger challenge was that even though Satan doesn't pray, he preys on those committed to prayer. He'd prefer a prayer-pretender to a genuine prayer warrior. If he can thwart our communication with Christ, setting us on a downward spiral, stymied by fear, then he has shattered our effectiveness for the Lord. The voice of Satan is one of reprimand, defeat, and hopelessness, preventing a child of the King from going to our Abba Father. Satan's goal is to keep Christians from claiming the biblical promise, "It was for freedom that Christ set us free."[65]

Is it any wonder then, that for some, creating time for prayer will always remain a disciplined battle, engaging the heavenly realms? Prayer won't just happen. Scheduling an appointment with God is essential because there is never enough time, an easier time, an opportune or convenient time, to pray.

To encourage us, A. W. Pink says, "Let us for a season gird up the loins of our minds and endeavor to contemplate Someone vastly different, Someone infinitely more excellent, namely, the One who is a total stranger to unrest and disquietude, the One who enjoys undisturbed calm, 'the God of peace.'"[66]

Paul's words instruct us, "Finally, be strong in the Lord and in the strength of His might. Put on the full armor of God, so that you will be able to stand firm against the schemes of the devil."[67] The only way we can victoriously enter the battleground of prayer is through the power of the Holy Spirit, clothed in the armor of God.

As I grew in my understanding about the complexity of prayer, I committed the following verses to memory.

"Therefore, take up the full armor of God, so that you will be able to resist in the evil day, and having done everything, to stand firm . . . having girded your loins with truth, and having put on the breastplate of righteousness, and having shod your feet with the preparation of the gospel of peace; in addition to all, taking up the shield of faith with which you will be able to extinguish all the flaming arrows of the evil one. And take the helmet of salvation, and the sword of the Spirit, which is the word of God."[68]

Paul's challenge to "stand firm," often catches me off guard. One such time was

January 2, 2012, when I experienced a brutal time of spiritual warfare. Within hours, I knew why. Here is a paraphrase of my journal entry: At 2:00 p.m., discouragement overcame me. By then I had been praying for four hours and my time communing with the Lord was sweet. But, between 2:00 and 3:30 p.m., I got several soliciting phone call interruptions. With no idea of what was going on, I felt a strong urge to abandon prayer and turn on the TV. A spiritual shroud of darkness overcame me for some unknown reason. I stuck with prayer until 3:30 p.m., but it was laborious. When such a feeling had occurred in the past, I just assumed my emotions shifted. But this time was different.

By 3:30 p.m., encouraging e-mails started appearing. People were thanking me for how encouraging my story was to them in their dark places. One quote said, "My husband and I just heard your testimony on the radio and were truly blessed." Another read, "When your story ended . . . I began to cry because of the joy in my heart . . . Your testimony encouraged me . . . Thank you so much for sharing your story; you have truly been a blessing."

Unbeknownst to me, between 2:00 and 3:00 p.m. in his nationally syndicated radio broadcast that day, Chris Fabry made the following comments to set up what he called "a best-of programs from October 2010":

> *You are a difference maker, your heart, your soul, your life. You are making a difference to those around you even if you don't sense it or understand it. . . . This program is going to make a difference in someone's life as we start off the New Year. . . . It deals with a woman who loved something, who had that thing she loved taken away from her and then instead of giving up, she allowed God to give her a new vision of that thing.*
>
> *One reason we wanted to air this in the first broadcast day of the New Year is because in the coming days and weeks, I want to look at people's lives who've been given a dream and who have allowed God to mold that dream in and through them. Because I'm convinced we can either hold on to the vision, the dream we have generated inside of us—what we think that ought to be, what we think life ought to be—or we can allow God to shape that in us to do what he wants. That's what the story of Alice Teisan is going to teach us today. That's what I hope you hear coming through loud and clear."[69]*

This episode was the first time I'd ever linked such feelings of resistance with fighting a war in the heavenly realm. Satan wanted me to end prematurely, making me believe my prayers were ineffective and just bouncing off the ceiling. The truth is, God was present. My prayers were bouncing off the airwaves around the country and the world via Internet and landing on the difficult places in people's hearts. From this experience, I recognized that in the future, when such resistance begins, I must stop and dress myself again in God's armor.

Was being on Chris Fabry's show that day a specific prayer of mine? No! It wasn't a quick Masada cable-car type of answer to prayer. This is an example of how we bring our petitions and intercessions to the Lord's throne repeatedly over the years. Here are three such prayers recorded in my journal: (1) May 8, 1998: "Use my pain and struggles to minister to others." (2) June 11, 2000: "Let me proclaim the hope of Christ dwelling within me to a world in need of hope." (3) June 16, 2000: "[During a conference, a leader prayed], 'God, commission Alice with your holy fire so she can go and speak truth where you send her.'" These prayers strengthened my Masada snake-path prayer walk.

The multifaceted nature of prayer is one that the passage from Ephesians 6, on the armor of God, goes on to explain. "With all prayer and petition pray at all times in the Spirit, and with this in view, be on the alert with all perseverance and petition for all the saints, and pray on my behalf, that utterance may be given to me in the opening of my mouth, to make known with boldness the mystery of the gospel, for which I am an ambassador in chains; that in proclaiming it I may speak boldly, as I ought to speak."[70]

For years, I had worn myself out serving Christ, and I didn't have time to spend with him. Could it be that one way in which Satan has dulled our ears to the Lord's voice is by causing us to believe that constant service for Christ equals intimacy with Christ? "My heart has heard you say, 'Come and talk with me.' And my heart responds, 'Lord, I am coming.'"[71]

Personal Prayer: God of Peace, I thank you for being the King of Kings and my Abba Father. Fine-tune my spiritual ears to discern your harmonious melody and Satan's dissonant noise. Help me to stand ready for battle suited in your armor—the belt of truth, the breastplate of righteousness, and my feet fitted with the gospel of peace. Thank you for the shield of faith, the helmet of salvation, the sword of the Spirit, and the Word of God as my protection (Ephesians 6:10-20). In the powerful name of my Savior, I pray. Amen.

QUESTIONS:

1. Identify the specific tactics the enemy uses to thwart your prayers.
2. What are some of the struggles you've experienced in prayer?
3. How have you seen your perseverance in prayer rewarded?
4. What Bible passage has enriched your prayers?

8

Boulders along the Path to Transformation

Only when the Holy Spirit renews, reeducates, and redirects our minds are we truly transformed.
—*Life Application Bible*, note on Romans 12:2

AS I HAD ENTERED into a deeper relationship with the Lord, it required ongoing examination of my heart. I memorized King David's words and prayed them often. "Search me, O God, and know my heart; Try me and know my anxious thoughts; and see if there be any hurtful way in me, and lead me in the everlasting way."[72]

Back in 1985, while taking an inventory of my heart before the Lord, I admitted my need for professional Christian counseling. One of the first statements I uttered in the counselor's office was, "I can't find joy in serving the Lord." Over time, I began to see that the service I was doing "for Christ" was masking my unmet needs and hidden emotions. Upon the recommendation of my counselor in 1989, I began attending a 12-step meeting. (See the twelve steps listed in the sidebar).

Anger was one of the boulders on my prayer ascent. The fourth step in the 12-step process requires making an inventory of resentments, but I didn't know where to begin. Somehow verbalizing anger was a cultural no-no within my evangelical milieu, having equated being a "good Christian" with never being angry. Impossible! Breaking free of this

12-Step Material	
1.	Admit powerlessness
2.	Find hope
3.	Surrender
4.	Take inventory
5.	Confess
6.	Become ready
7.	Ask God
8.	Make a list of amends
9.	Make amends
10.	Continue my inventory
11.	Pray and meditate
12.	Help others

lifetime self-deception would require lots of onerous plodding.

One of the helpful tools for looking at my anger was an emotion-feeling word chart that listed them according to intensity (low, medium, or high). In conjunction with the chart, I memorized a Scripture verse that I began to apply: "Be angry, and yet do not sin; do not let the sun go down on your anger."[73] Another component was working through the 12-step program within a small group. While making an inventory of resentments, I used lists of categories provided in the material which covered all the areas where a person could hold a grudge. Overarching categories such as people, institutions, and principles were then broken down with a variety of examples.

To assist me in identifying what was going on inside. I began using some 12-step resources as prayer prompters. On February 27, 1989, I wrote, "I'm feeling terribly stressed out . . . I'm sad that I'm so busy. It feels uncomfortable, unsociable, and crazy. I'm unable to get out of an automatic pilot mode." On March 6, "I'm scared; I feel like I'm going 1,000 miles a minute." On November 14, I laid my heart bare to the Lord, articulating a fear around my heart's desire, "I won't ever get a job with a bike company. You've got to be someone special, and I'm not special." Ouch!

Also in 1989, I joined a group study focused around Evelyn Christenson's book *What Happens When Women Pray*,[74] complementing the soul-care I had already begun. It contained instructions on how to integrate reading Scripture, meeting weekly, and praying together. While working through the study, I developed a stronger hunger for prayer as I got a glimpse of its power.

Redefining prayer as something other than an instant handout approach to all my demanding requests was central to building intimacy with Christ. A quick daily devotional time of reading Scripture and speedily blurting out a need as if he were the man in a red suit, with a white beard, and fat belly, dispensing my vending machine requests, wasn't reality. I knew it, but I still had a long road ahead before I could transition to a place of being quiet in his presence while embracing God as gloriously strong, and my Abba Father. After beginning to face the anger in my life, it started showing up everywhere. My prayer journal entry from March 8 read, "I'm angry with God for allowing a dating relationship to end!" I knew we were incompatible, but that didn't stop me from being angry.

Another meaningful scriptural promise I clung to during this vulnerable time was, "You will know the truth, and the truth will set you free."[75] The Lord continues uncovering the ugliness and painful truth about the sinful behaviors in my life. Moreover, when they have been uncovered, I've often reacted with a defensive spirit before recognizing my own vulnerability to his loving but firm rebuke. Humility combined with submission is part of the process of dying to my will and grasping hold of his ways.

One such sinful behavior the Lord exposed around anger was my dishonesty by silence. Remaining silent and not sharing my thoughts or opinions wasn't a godly act of holding my tongue. Instead, by doing so I was being dishonest through silent omission. I brought this same action to my prayer time, remaining silent; fearing what would happen if I voiced the negative thoughts that I had toward the Lord or others.

I recognized that anger could take many different paths. One life-draining route is depression, anger turned inward against myself. Common patterns of depressive anger that I experienced included blaming myself for another person's unhappiness or problem. I also internalized the lie that I didn't deserve good things from God. I analyzed and rehashed everything I said, while demeaning myself. Anything negative that occurred within my family or in my presence I automatically internalized and believed, "It was all my fault and I was to blame." These demoralizing lies and passive-aggressive forms of control stole my joy. I now see that depression, as a medical manifestation of anger, is also a rampant problem within the church and throughout our society.

God used my counselor to help me identify how sarcasm, besides silence, had become my "appropriate" method of venting anger, obstructing healthy communication with God and others. Months later on October 19, 1989, while praying, I wrote, "I'm learning to accept the good things, and not belittle them. Using sarcasm isn't something I can continue doing."

Removing the boulder of anger required working through step five—confession. Once I understood my part, I was responsible to seek forgiveness from God and others, confessing my dishonesty through silence. My sin resulted in some painful consequences—such as strained relationships and lost friendships, but confession was necessary.

Through this discovery process, my relationship with God was also moving closer to an Abba Father type of intimacy, putting the words of James into action. "For the anger of man does not achieve the righteousness of God. Therefore, putting aside all filthiness and *all* that remains of wickedness, in humility receive the word implanted, which is able to save your souls."[76]

At times, from the outside observer's viewpoint, the emotional and spiritual mess appeared as if I were just drudging up painful issues with no solutions. Friends would periodically ask, "Why are you reading all those books? What good does it do?" These questions at times left me doubting my journey.

Here is a prayer I wrote during this season: "May I know I am not giving something up, I am getting filled up from the heavenly storehouse of blessings, which are mine. Am I willing to invest and seek hard after them?" The excitement that bubbled up in my heart confirmed that I was going the right way—along the Masada snake-path prayer ascent. Again, on March 12, in a cathartic dark hole, I wrote, "Jesus Christ is the only one I plan to be indebted to for life."

Accepting myself in light of whom the sovereign Lord created me to be as stated in Psalm 139 was fundamental. "My frame was not hidden from You, When I was made in secret, and skillfully wrought in the depths of the earth; Your eyes have seen my unformed substance; and in Your book were all written. The days that were ordained for me, when as yet there was not one of them."[77] Only when tackling the arduous boulders in my deceitful heart—turning from complacency, sentimentality, pessimism, acedia (spiritual or mental apathy), etc.—and obediently following God's path, am I putting forgiveness into action. All too often I've been guilty of taking the first step of asking for forgiveness, from God or others, and then omitting the required next step of changing my ways. Nevertheless, I was learning that faith in action was required if I wanted to bring glory to God and continue building a genuine relationship with him through prayer, and consequentially with others.

Personal Prayer: Mighty Counselor, I approach your throne. Search me and know my heart, try me and know my anxious thoughts. Uncover the sinful ways within my deceitful heart (Psalm 139:23-24).

As you do, give me the courage to confess my sins to you and to those I've offended. Clothed in your forgiveness, grant me the courage to seek forgiveness from the one I've sinned against. I pray all these things in the cleansing blood of the Lamb. Amen.

QUESTIONS:

1. How do you take inventory of your heart?
2. Who holds you accountable?
3. What are some unhealthy ways in which anger, resentment, or other sin has manifested itself?
4. What are some of the steps you have taken to deal with your anger?

9

The Spectacular in the Ordinary

The holy eye is the one who is able to see the extraordinary beauties of
the ordinary days!
—Mehmet Murat ildan

REFLECTING ON THE ONGOING longing for a rich prayer
life, I remembered the summer of 1983, when I got a taste of
what I had hoped to experience in the future. It was between my
junior and senior years of nursing school. The place was Zimbabwe,
Africa, while on a nine-week student missionary project with The
Evangelical Alliance Mission (TEAM). The plan was for me to work
in a TEAM-run bush clinic. My purpose was to explore whether
foreign missions was something I sensed God leading me to pursue
as a full-time career.

Due to extenuating circumstances, the initial plans were
changed. Instead, I worked with Scripture Union and Youth for
Christ, the national branch of these international parachurch

69

Christian youth organizations. As a result, I had the privilege of living with Tobias and Rose Nyatsambo and their three school-aged children. Years earlier, Tobias worked full time with Scripture Union as a regional director responsible for schools and camps. Rose was an elementary school teacher. Tobias had done his undergraduate work in Britain. In addition, the family was versed in cross-cultural communication, and fluent in both English and Shona.

While working with the Zimbabwean nationals in these two ministries, it struck me how the whole office stopped working at 10:30 a.m. Everyone gathered for a thirty- to forty-five-minute midmorning tea (a sacred occurrence since Zimbabwe was once a British colony) and prayer time. Coworkers gave praise. Prayers were offered for the mundane, "Thank you, Lord, that the electricity is working today." *What?* I thought! *Praying for electricity? I've never prayed for the electricity to run. That's Commonwealth Edison's responsibility.* A routine operation prayer was, "Lord, we have phone calls this afternoon that we need to make. Please help the phones to work." *What?* I thought. *How dare that my phone should quit on me. I paid for AT&T to provide such services, so if it fails they are the ones I'd call and complain to about the problem. I wouldn't bother God with such an issue; that wasn't his problem!*

The team also covered upcoming events in prayer, such as the logistics and ministry issues. Each day we would get a report on the number of campers who had signed up for the upcoming camp. Then we'd pray for each registrant and for God to fill the open slots. I sensed the entire staff knew their ministries were dependent on prayer, and apart from it there was no way of sustaining work.

One particular afternoon, I was to venture out alone for an appointment. During midmorning prayer, prior to my leaving, the staff prayed for traveling safety—specifically, that the directions they had provided, along with God's help, would get me to and from my appointment.

Before even starting, I had four strikes against me. (1) First time driving a stick shift unsupervised and never having done so with the stick on the steering column. (2) First time driving on the left side of the road. (3) No idea where I was going and no internet for directions back then. (4) One of the aftermaths of the war was stolen street signs, which Zimbabwe had experienced in 1980, three years prior.

While driving to my appointment, I made a wide left-hand turn as if I were driving on the right side of the road. What could have ended in a major accident only received the honk of a horn from the oncoming driver in front of me. God was answering the teatime prayers! Then as I turned down the street without a sign, somehow it resonated in my heart that God was leading. How, you may ask? Well, I know the disconcerting voice that replays in my head about 90 percent of the time. It goes like this, *Oh, why did you do something so stupid?* Or, in this instance, it would have been something like, *You can't even follow directions, can you?* For the other 10 percent of the time, when I experience constructive, encouraging thoughts that make sense going through my head, I know where they stem from—the Lord. What makes sense often puts me out of my comfort zone—just like driving and turning down a street without a sign.

I like how John Gill, a commentator from 1800, has explained a verse that addresses God speaking to a person, "And the LORD replied, 'Do as they say, and give them a king.'"[78] Gill says, "By an audible voice, or by an impulse upon his mind."[79] I've never had God speak to me in an audible voice, but I can relate to receiving an impulse upon my mind.

After safely returning, I reflected on God's presence in every detail of my travels, and I knew he had answered my colleagues' prayers for safety, direction, and protection. I paused and considered, *Do I pray for the mundane, my daily needs, and agenda back home?* Truth was I never really felt I needed to depend on God's answers as I did that day. I couldn't get enough prayer time with these leaders. I had never before experienced the power of prayer in such a tangible way.

When debriefing the nine weeks I spent in Zimbabwe, I didn't sense overseas missionary nursing was the way God wanted me to use my professional talents. It became clear how I was to participate in missions—by providing tools for national workers to help themselves. At the time, I couldn't fathom such a concept. What did it mean? Where would I get the idea? How could I do such a thing? All these unanswered questions, and more, didn't make me feel like I was any closer to participating in missions.

Frightened, I wondered, *Can I only encounter the real Lord through prayer if I return to Africa as a full-time missionary? Will I ever find a powerful prayer life for myself at home?* It seemed to me that the Christian leaders in Zimbabwe had a deeper reliance and trust in prayer than the Christian leaders I'd met in America. I prayerfully pondered, *What do I need in my life before I can create a helpful prayer environment?*

It had been brewing in my heart as evidence by the verse I picked for my prayer card before going to Zimbabwe. "Then I said, 'Alas, Lord GOD! Behold, I do not know how to speak, because I am a youth.' But the LORD said to me, 'Do not say, 'I am a youth,' because everywhere I send you, you shall go, and all that I command you, you shall speak.'"[80]

Never before had I experienced a daily midmorning prayer gathering, even within Christian organizations. I wondered, *Is this because of our culture's mindset—viewing time as money? Or when unable to grasp the unseen productivity of prayer, we deem it a worthless endeavor?*

When thinking about the Zimbabwean lifestyle, it appeared much simpler than the fast-paced way of life, to which I'd grown accustomed. For instance, they didn't have as many extracurricular activities beyond school and work. In addition, extended families ate meals together on a regular basis. There were enough amenities to make life comfortable without the excessive material things, including electronic gadgetry, which these days (2017), vie for any spare moments.

With gas being so expensive, they planned their travel and their holidays (vacation time) closer to home. One reason was they couldn't take more than three hundred dollars a year, per adult, out of the country. It was incomprehensible to think that if such a rule could apply to the USA, we wouldn't be allowed take more than three hundred dollars a year out of the state, or even order something by mail from another state. With a roof over their heads and their daily needs supplied, their main dependence was prayer, a reliance on the King of All Resources.

As Tobias said, "Prayer is a relationship that comes out of trust, and not entitlement. Life is a daily surprise and this includes even the gift from a neighbor. In our culture, God is real; and each day (and each daily need supplied) is to be celebrated. Prayer never produced spectacular responses or answers but changed us to see the spectacular, the hand of God, in the ordinary." How I longed to experience the spectacular hand of God in my everyday ordinary reality.

I wanted to believe I relied on the Lord when I prayed. But I had to admit that my main dependence was upon material resources. Then a full-time nursing student, I probably prayed for financial resources, but making a phone call home seemed to have a quicker response—money sent to me should I even fear running out! My parents weren't rich, but had given me the gift of paying for my education. It was much easier for me to rely on the tangible help from my parents than to believe in the foreign alternative of prayer. All too often as Americans, since our material needs are met in other ways, we don't take time to pray until we have difficulties that we can't fix—illness, death, great sorrows, etc.

Over the next five years (1983–1988), after returning from Zimbabwe, I mulled over the question, *Was the power of prayer something for the Africans only, or could I find such a reliance on God?* I would need to simplify my life before I could create space for prayer.

My Zimbabwean prayer encounter created a quandary. It seems that many in the United States have believed a lie—we claim he is a sovereign Lord, and yet we pray as if he is subordinate. This attitude permeates our Western culture, including within our church walls. It stymies our belief that prayer can make a difference in our lives, the lives around us, or worldwide. Over time, I asked myself, *Will I accept such a cultural norm, found even within the American evangelical denominational practices, as my own biblical perspective on prayer? No!* I longed to pray with a conviction that the words of Psalm 108 were true: "With God we shall do valiantly, it is He who will tread down our foes."[81]

Thanks to the rich, powerful prayer experience mirrored by the Zimbabweans, I am now able to recognize how deceived I had been by thinking financial provisions could replace carving out time for prayer back home. I knew God longed to do much more in my life, through my life, and beyond my life, but first I needed to become serious about spending my life communing with him. Through time, I'm learning that prayer opens the lens of our soul to view the mundane of each day as the magnanimous and the ordinary unveils the spectacular of the sovereign One.

Personal Prayer: Almighty God, I am thankful that you want to work valiantly through me (Psalm 108:13). Thank you for the obedience to trust your Word back in 1983: "Alas, Lord GOD! Behold, I do not know how to speak, because I am a youth." But the Lord said to me, "Everywhere I send you, you shall go, and all that I command you, you shall speak." Thank you for your Word, which is my compass, and "a lamp to my feet and a light to my path" (Psalm 119:05). With a grateful heart, I thank you, the Sun of Righteousness. Amen.

QUESTIONS:

1. What is an excuse or obstacle that keeps you from plugging into the power of prayer?
2. Describe what it was like to experience an intensely close time in God's presence.
3. What role models do you have for a deeper prayer life?

4. What is a scripture verse that has been your compass?

10

Barriers Can Be Blessings

*Affliction . . . does not bereave of hope, but recruits hope. For affliction
compels the person mercilessly to let go of everything else, that he may
learn to grasp the eternal and hang on to the eternal.*
—Soren Kierkegaard

IN 1992, I FACED what seemed the strongest barriers to prayer.
On July 23, 1992, the countdown had begun. Only four days left
before the start of a ten-day, 1,000-mile bike trip. It was the first step
toward actualizing a dream of working with Wandering Wheels, the
bicycle organization I had cycled with since 1977.

The day began like any other, getting ready for my home health
nursing duties, when flu-like symptoms wiped me out. Vertigo caused
the room to spin, such that I slithered to the phone and called my
supervisor, "I'm too sick to work."

From there I crawled to my bedroom, and after awaking from a
nap, I called Wandering Wheels. When Sue, the office manager,

answered I said, "I woke up this morning with what I think is the twenty-four-hour flu. I don't foresee any change in plans, but I will keep you posted."

Worsening symptoms accompanied each passing day, forcing me to cancel my trip on the sixth day. Bone-deep pain took up residence in every sinew and fiber of my being, chasing away even the illusion of restorative sleep. It was a struggle to walk the few feet from my bedroom to the bathroom and on to the kitchen for nourishment, only to find the cupboard, fridge, and freezer almost bare, prior to vacation.

The same day I got sick, the 1992 Summer Olympics began. Having dreamed of one day having time to watch them, I allowed it to consume the few hours each day I could sit up. After two days of this mind-numbing extravaganza, I was bored, having never really enjoyed TV. I thought, *I don't know how long this illness is going to last, but I still want my life to count for something.* That day I revised my prayer plan since 1988 from one uninterrupted hour of prayer a week to one hour a day.

At this Masada snake-path trailhead of another kind, I thought about the stones of remembrance I had intentionally set down while in Israel in 1988, when my spiritual light was shining bright: (1) Rededicating my life to the Lord in the Jordan River, where I vowed, *God, I will go with you from now on, wherever you lead;* (2) Vowing, "Never forget God, never again!" after carrying my bike to the top of Masada, the spiritual fortress; and (3) Deciding to intentionally pursue prayer four months after returning home from Israel.

Now, pleading for health and healing consumed my prayer time as days melted into weeks that blurred into unending months. My symptoms included a low-grade fever, bone-deep pain, brain fog, delayed reaction time, and increased sensitivity to sound, light, and temperature. Once able to exercise regularly, I found now even minimal exertion created a forty-eight- to seventy-two-hour relapse. My calendar days previously filled with work, workouts, and church activities now consisted of endless doctor's appointments, blood draws, and other medical procedures. The only thing reliable about me now was being unreliable.

Single and living alone, I feared, *Will this illness steal my independence and force me to move out of my Chicago apartment and return to my parents' home in Detroit?* Just caring for the activities of daily living—preparing meals and trying to find restorative sleep—was overwhelming. When the curtain of paralyzing confusion lifted, it ushered in more questions. *What's wrong with me? Is my condition terminal? Will I live, die, or ever work again?*

Weeks after getting sick, I went from a full-time nursing position to short-term disability. Three months later, in October 1992, after returning my home health nursing supplies and employee identification card, I reached a critical juncture—long-term total disability. The status change made me feel as if I were no longer viewed as a productive member of society.[82]

During this traumatic time, I was grateful for the instructions in the book of Joshua. He instructed the Israelites, whose faith was faltering then like mine was now, to "Pass on before the ark of the LORD your God into the midst of the Jordan, and take up each of you a stone upon his shoulder . . . a sign among you. When your children ask . . . 'What do those stones mean to you?' then you shall tell them that the waters of the Jordan were cut off before the ark of the covenant of the LORD. . . . These stones shall be . . . a memorial forever."[83]

As agonizing months toppled into an uncertain future, while questioning God, I needed these stones of his faithful remembrance. *Why me? What have I done wrong? Aren't I entitled to a healthy, easy life?* Troubled, I pleaded for answers. *Could a loving God really allow me to fall sick and become so weak and unproductive at the age of thirty, in the prime of my youth?* As I tried to grapple with what had become a chronic illness, I faced yet another stage of grieving—the "re-evaluation of life, roles and goals"[84] as I fretted, *Will I ever fulfill my dream to lead bicycle trips, to have the health needed to resume any semblance of the life I'd once known? Alternatively, has life as I've known it ceased to exist?* I acted upon my Jordan River vow—*God, I will go with you from now on, wherever you lead.* Dealing with these concerns was part of the long road to the acceptance of suffering, my newfound intimate companion, along with its newfound limitations.

I felt like suffering was truly a prayer barrier; and then I was confronted with the second half of Philippians 3:10, a verse I had picked during my teenage years. The first part described my longing, "To know Christ—yes, to know the power of his resurrection." But as each day passed without any health improvements, I struggled. *Was "participation in his sufferings" part of the formula to "becoming like him in his death"?* Suffering causes me to fantasize about an easier road of transformation—a quick Masada cable-car excursion. Yet I know that acknowledging the truth of a situation is foundational for discovering biblical hope. I wondered, *If suffering made Christ the great sympathizer, could it be that suffering, instead of being a barrier, would deepen my intimacy with him and prepare me to sympathize with others in their distress?*

An American cultural barrier to prayer is productivity. How else would I measure prayer effectiveness and productivity but by instant gratification—answers to my prayers. *Would prayer ever compare to all the valuable commitments I did for you, Lord, at church and work before my health ended? Did you forget the way you wired me and the dreams and passions you instilled within me?*

An example of my productivity prayer barrier, which others may experience, was manifest as a rigid prayer plan, a task, even a prayer competition of sorts. I'd see how many people's issues I could rattle off during prayer: a way to quantify the value and worth of my productivity! *Keep my family safe, give them good health, and bless my friends.* The habit of racing through such a checklist was an intimacy-squelching roadblock that was similar to the productivity performance expectations in my home health nursing position. Throughout the long months, I struggled, *God, would you ever use the pain and loss from my disability for your glory and your Kingdom purposes?*

In April 1993, after nine months of battling pain and inner struggle, and having seen nineteen different specialists, I heard a verdict during a visit to my internist. "You have Myalgic Encephalomyelitis/Chronic Fatigue Syndrome (ME/CFS)!" For an instant, knowing I had a diagnosis, I felt a twinge of relief until my brain processed the words. Then my heart sank, as if a judge had delivered my life sentence and thrown away the key. Other names for the condition included "yuppie flu" and "shirker syndrome" (declared when a person decides to shirk their daily responsibilities). It's also been known as Chronic Fatigue Immune Dysfunction Syndrome, pronounced C-Feds; and as of 2015, the newest name is Systemic Exertion Intolerance Disease. No matter what you call it, as a nurse I knew ME/CFS was real and that it had created a real problem—a medical mystery void of answers! Laura Hillenbrand states, "The word fatigue is to this disease as a match is to a nuclear bomb. It simply does not come close to describing what you experience."[85]

"At a congressional briefing (1995), Mark Loveless, M.D., an infectious disease specialist and head of the AIDS and ME/CFS Clinic at Oregon Health Sciences University, testified that a ME/CFS[86] patient feels every day effectively the same as an AIDS patient feels two months before death."[87] Dr. Nancy Klimas, a leading ME/CFS researcher said, "My H.I.V. patients for the most part are hale and hearty, thanks to three decades of intense and excellent research and billions of dollars invested. Many of my ME/CFS patients, on the other hand, are terribly ill and unable to work or participate in the care of their families. I split my clinical time between the two illnesses, and I can tell you if I had to choose between the two illnesses I would rather have H.I.V (2009)."[88] Moreover, as someone said, "ME/CFS takes your life away, but it doesn't have the courtesy to kill you."[89] On June 1, 2106, Ryan Prior, who founded the "The Blue Ribbon Fellowship" to further practical ME/CFS healthcare education for students studying in infectious disease, refers to CFS/ME as the "Forgotten Plague." He says, "A recent survey of 119 medical textbooks showed that information on Chronic Fatigue Syndrome or Myalgic encephalomyelitis was presented on just 0.9 percent of medical textbook pages. It showed that the illness is significantly underrepresented in medical textbooks compared with diseases that are much less prevalent such as Lyme disease and multiple sclerosis."[90]

In the midst of my turmoil, I longed for the day that my heart would pulsate with his during prayer. *Will I ever find enjoyment in being with the Lord and charting undiscovered territory?* I sure hoped so, but I have to confess prayer felt more like a duty than a gift. *How will I pray an hour a day? And how will I pray without falling asleep?* As I faced these barriers, my stone of remembrance—Never forget God, Never again—helped me forge ahead.

There were other barriers too. I confess it is easier to make time for absurd distractions like the two-day Summer Olympics TV extravaganza, or "just making one more phone call," than making God my first priority. It was then I made two decisions: one was to limit my TV time to the evening news and a game show or two, and the other was to decrease the number of phone calls I made a day.

Even though I knew the phone was a distraction, I still succumbed to hearing an audible voice and thus answering the phone, because communicating with an invisible God felt less real. But every time I answered, the intimate, quiet place vanished. Additional interruptions that have grown over the years include surfing the web, chatting on social media, and retrieving e-mails. Back in 1992, I didn't own a computer and the World Wide Web was only a year old. Allowing these distractions to take priority over prayer speaks volumes—no worries, God will still be available when I finally have time for him. Of course, he understands!

Another barrier I've been haunted by during prayer is a brain response that mimicked the picture on an old TV screen. One minute I had a clear reception with my Holy Spirit-ual Director, followed by a whiteout blizzard—zero visibility, signal gone. During that time doubts raged! *Why am I sitting here trying to pray when I can't even think? How can I reconnect with God's signal? Am I giving God my best? If not now, then why not stop and resume later when I can?*

This led me to wonder, *Is there a perfect time to pray? Is praying early in the morning synonymous with giving God the best time of my day? Did it guarantee the reward of a sweeter, more intimate time with the Lord?* I sure hoped not! Since ME/CFS, makes sleep nearly impossible and the thought of rising early is unbearable.

While building my prayer muscle in 1992, I wish I had understood this aid to overcoming barriers that Matthew Henry so eloquently penned: "It is a transfiguring, transforming duty. By prayer we fetch in the wisdom, grace, and joy, which make the face to shine."[91] Another prayer warrior, George Mueller, wrote, "A HUMAN life, filled with the presence and power of God, is one of God's choicest gifts to His church and to the world."[92] In 2013, I wrote, *Is the power in prayer and the miracle of prayer reason enough for me to keep praying?* Yes! Prayer "is reason enough."

Prior to becoming disabled, I lived an active lifestyle, giving minimal attention to proper spiritual care. I never imagined the freedom, joy, and power lying dormant, waiting to be awakened and explored through prayer.

When ME/CFS struck, I experienced repeated losses; overwhelming gloom surrounded my sickbed and threatened to crumble the foundation of my faith. It was for such a time as this that

I was reminded of the promise I made in the Jordan River, "God, I will go with you from now on, wherever you lead." In a spiritually healthy place when I vowed, "Never forget God, never again" I didn't know then how many times I'd need to rely on this reminder when circumstances have overwhelmed me and threatened to snuff out my spiritual light. I'm grateful for the spiritual anchor, the decision I made soon after returning from Israel in 1998, to make prayer my number one occupation. It was long before the undercurrent of a chronic disability left me wondering if my life still had purpose. I've needed all my stones of remembrances, tangible personalized reminders of God's care, the ones I identified in spiritually bright times, as my constant companions through the difficult days along my spiritual path.

Personal Prayer: Father of Light, I thank you for holding my hand and guiding me along life's path. Thank you, Lord, that the instructions you gave the Israelites are still relevant practices today—gathering stones of remembrance. You have cared for me and intervened on my behalf in so many ways. Forgive me for being so quick to question your protection when facing trials. Lord Jesus, I choose today to cling to you, my Shepherd. Amen.

QUESTIONS:
1. What is one of your prayer barriers?
2. What distractions keep you from praying?
3. Tell about one of your spiritual stones of remembrance that you have collected.

11

Disguised Gifts

*No one should give the answer that it is impossible for a man occupied
with worldly cares to pray always. You can set up an altar to God in
your mind by means of prayer. And so it is fitting to pray at your
trade, on a journey, standing at a counter or sitting at your handicraft.*
—St John Chrysostom

IN MAY 1993, TEN months after ME/CFS struck, even though
the barriers continued, I was feeling strong enough to return to
work as a nurse. The Cardiac Rehabilitation Department at West
Suburban Hospital, where I had worked part time since 1988, had an
opening for twelve hours a week, spread out over three four-hour
shifts. By early 1994, I was able to work my way up to about twenty
hours a week as I felt better and as a few more hours opened up.

By 1996, still facing obstacles, functioning at only about 50
percent, I fought to resume a few social activities, including taking
guitar lessons at Chicago's Old Town School of Folk Music. Then

one hot April day in 1996, while doing rehab with a patient in the intensive care unit (ICU), the cubicle started to spin. I stepped out for some air when one of the ICU nurses noticed me. Seeing my flushed face as I wobbled and swayed, while I sweated profusely and struggled to answer simple questions, she assisted me to a chair. There she performed a nursing assessment, and minutes later, I was wheeled to the emergency room (ER).

Once in the ER, my heart continued speeding, leaving my energy tank on empty, which created a sneaking suspicion. When the EKG, vitals, and blood work came back normal, it confirmed my deepest fear—a ME/CFS relapse. This led to repeated losses, of which one was returning to full-time disability, not knowing then that I'd never work again as a nurse.

Weeks later, I underwent a tilt table test, which began by lying still on an X-ray table. After the technician hooked me up to the EKG machine and took my resting vital signs, she tilted the table to an upright position. Within thirty seconds of being in the standing position without moving, my heart rate went from 90 to160—the first test in four years that showed any abnormality. Nevertheless, it would take another ten years before any physician would properly manage postural orthostatic tachycardia syndrome (POTS), a secondary diagnosis common with ME/CFS. "Research shows that POTS patients' quality of life is similar to those with congestive heart failure and chronic obstructive pulmonary disease."[93] I was a cardiac rehabilitation nurse, certified as an exercise specialist through the American College of Sports Medicine. I held a degree in kinesiology, was athletic, and wrote exercise prescriptions for those with chronic medical conditions—yet I was stricken with idiopathic (unknown cause) exercise intolerance.

One of the first attempts at treating the condition was beta-blockers, which brought my heart rate down so low I could hardly get out of bed. Not knowing what was happening created severe depression. These hidden disabilities also created the added complexity and grief of having to fight to be understood, which is physically exhausting. Many within the healthcare system, and outside of it, doubt if ME/CFS is a legitimate condition, instead wanting to label it as depression. "Leonard Jason, a professor of psychology at DePaul University in Chicago and a widely-respected ME/CFS researcher, said that a good strategy for distinguishing between the illness and depression is to ask patients what they would do if they suddenly recovered. Those suffering from a major depressive disorder, he said, would likely say they didn't know. 'But someone with ME/CFS would probably begin making lists of all the things that they wanted to do,' he said."[94] I agree—my waiting list is already extensive!

POTS made standing in a checkout line nearly impossible and created the same set of symptoms when I was sitting in a warm room, above 68 degrees, for any length of time. But it would take ten years of detective work to figure out why I would get sick in some buildings and not others. No longer able to live alone, I moved out of the Chicago apartment I had rented for seven years and began sharing a house with two other women.

Amid this health upheaval, I tried to stay true to my prayer plan, and even increased my time to two hours a day. However, bedbound, "with all the time in the world," didn't make prayer any easier or obstacle free. Settling into prayer often mimicked the struggle of putting a toddler down for a nap. I'd whine and mentally kick and scream, *God, I'm too sick to pray. I don't even have the strength to get out of bed. What are the relationship rules and guidelines for prayer? I don't care about you right now because I'm not convinced you are listening to my prayers.* I never ran out of prayer excuses, and my ranting magnified my grumpy heart.

Then while grieving the losses I experienced from ME/CFS, the life-shaping question God asked Moses came to mind. "What is that in your hand?"[95] Moses answered, "A staff." I wondered, *Was Moses perplexed by the question and shocked by the exchange that followed?* God said, "Throw it on the ground." Moses obeyed and the staff became "a serpent, and Moses ran from it. But the LORD said to Moses, 'Stretch out your hand and grasp it by its tail'—so he stretched out his hand and caught it, and it became a staff in his hand—"[96]

Subconsciously I had hoped prayer was equivalent to playing "my Masada cable-car, get-well-quick-card." When I relinquished my illness to the Lord, then he'd not delay in performing the scripted part I'd written for him—healing me completely, and not dillydallying as he did with Moses! But it didn't happen my way. And I lacked the energy to carry on the prayer time as I once did, talking incessantly, a turbulent, babbling brook of propaganda crashing into the Almighty King of Kings. I grumbled, *Is prayer ALL I can do? What kind of impossible gift have you placed in my hand and etched on my heart?* It caused me to pause and consider what Moses must have thought, "A staff! So what?"

On September 27, 1997, while visiting Jen, my dear friend from nursing school, I found her busy with her three children under the age of five. Her husband Solano was preparing to pour a cement slab for playing basketball. And I was off in another room having a prayer pity party; *God, I feel too sick to help! What can I do?*

During my complaining, God uncovered a deep-seated envy in my heart. I longed for the energy and strength that God had given Jen—health, family, and a busy schedule. In my funk, I hadn't considered that God gave Jen a different hand, the one she'd need to face the challenges that accompanied her "blessings"; one was navigating the family issues that present themselves when raising a son with disabilities. Now God highlighted the special gifts he had given me that were different from Jen's but equally valuable, even though it took time to accept—singlehood, living alone, and the silence for praying without interruptions. In the movie *Karate Kid*, Jackie Chan's character, Mr. Han, addresses my misunderstanding: "Being still and doing nothing are two very different things."[97] With time, prayer has become an important component of my daily rhythm, a compass for directing my decision-making process, and a way of turning loneliness into solitude.

The longer I sat alone, the stronger God nudged me, *Offer to help Solano!* I grumbled, *I have nothing to offer.* However, God didn't accept my argument! Finally, still thinking, *God, you know there's nothing I can do,* I got off the couch and found Solano. My stinky attitude made me wonder, *How did Moses respond? Did he struggle with a bad attitude, or did he respond with a willing spirit?*

"Is there anything I can do to help?" I asked Solano. "Would you go to the hardware store and buy an eighteen-inch cement tool?" he asked. *Ugh, that tool isn't sufficient for the job,* I thought. *What a useless errand.* But off I went to the rural Bronson, Michigan hardware store, poor attitude and all, yet knowing the tool was all Solano could afford.

When I couldn't find the tool, I sought out the sales clerk for help. He asked, "What type of cement project are you doing?" As I began to explain, a man overhearing our conversation interrupted "The eighteen-inch troll isn't adequate for the job." Inside I screamed, *I know,* as he continued, "I'm a cement contractor and my barn's only a mile down the road. I will loan you all the necessary tools to do the job right."

Having grown up in Detroit and now living in Chicago, I drove to his barn thinking, *I must be crazy having agreed to follow this stranger.*

After loading more than $1,000 worth of proper tools into my car, the contractor asked, "What's your name and where do you live?" I paused, "Ahhh, my name is Alice Teisan and I live in the Chicagoland area. I'm visiting the Araujos—pronounced Ah-da-oo-jus, friends who moved here three years ago from Brazil." His face went blank, as if thinking, *What have I just done?* as he rubbed his hand across his tightly knit brow. He probably had assumed I was related to someone he knew in Bronson. Attempting to calm his fears, I gave him three local contacts before saying, "Umm, I'm returning to Chicago tomorrow, but I promise you'll get your tools back on time!"

On the drive back to the Araujos', I prayed, asking the Lord to forgive me for my whining, thinking I knew how everything was going to turn out. Through this encounter, two verses have become more personal to me: "To obey is better than sacrifice."[98] And, "My God will supply all your needs according to His riches in glory in Christ Jesus."[99]

For the longest time, I assumed the sinful issues that surface during prayer in the form of spiritual temper tantrums meant I wasn't being "holy" enough. What I'm learning is that prayer and pity parties often go together. It is here the Holy Spirit-ual Director uses Scripture to shine the light of truth upon sin, as Hebrews records. "The word of God is living and active and sharper than any two-edged sword, and piercing as far as the division of soul and spirit . . . able to judge the thoughts and intentions of the heart . . . all things are open and laid bare to the eyes of Him."[100] Acknowledging and then naming our sinful behaviors is part of the confessional process of dying to self and meeting Christ at the cross, the crux of healing and wholeness— where transformation and freedom occur.

Even though God was capable of allowing the Israelites to take the direct, Masada cable-car life route, he was more concerned with their spiritual formation than their physical comfort. I don't want to wander in the wilderness of ME/CFS for forty years! Nevertheless, Moses' story highlights that God isn't in a hurry. Answered prayer isn't my way only! Instead, a spiritual growth and development route provides a backdrop for the Lord's majestic display of glory.

Where once I assumed it was my job to fill up all the prayer space, now I know the ultimate act of prayer is intentionality in turning away from distractions and yielding my heart and circumstances to the Lord. Each time I say yes to God, I surrender a little more of my hands, heart, and life to him. The gift of prayer placed in my hands has also become a conduit of blessing to others.

Personal Prayer: I come before you saying, Holy, Holy, Holy are you, Lord God Almighty. Thank you for your Word, which is living and active and sharper than any two-edged sword (Hebrews 4:12). I choose to accept my suffering as a valuable asset. Please use all that is in my hands and etched on my heart as you used Moses' hand to display your glory and power. Thank you, Jesus, for the power-filled gift of prayer. Amen!

QUESTIONS:

1. What is in your hand, etched on your heart, or tattooed on your skin that God wants to use? Look at Exodus 4:1-4.
2. What are you envying that is in someone else's hand?
3. How does God want to use you for his glory?

12

A New Dose of Energy

The contemplative life generates and releases an enormous amount of energy into the world—the enlivening energy of God's grace rather than the enervating frenzy of our pride.
—Eugene Peterson

AS MY HEALTH CONTINUED faltering throughout the remaining months of 1996, I brought my grief and depression to the cross, *"the great organ of Divine power."*[101] Prayer didn't magically take away my depression, but since isolation, depression, and hopelessness are common among those with ME/CFS, it made my spiritual Masada even more important. Dr. David McKay, a clinical psychologist and professor at Trinity Seminary, helped me to navigate the sharp edges of grief, loss, and altered self-image on the dark road of my illness. As time went by, psychological help wasn't enough. Whenever I experienced another physical relapse, my emotions began to unravel.

My outward appearance was one of strength and health, but I was unable to regain my internal balance. Finally, at a 1996 appointment with the endocrinologist, he said, "There is more to life than a good heart rate and healthy blood pressure. I think it's time for an antidepressant and antianxiety medication. By the time you've come to this point with ME/CFS and tachycardia [elevated heart rate], you have been through Hell."[102] The orders to see a psychiatrist caused me to ache with still another type of pain . . .

When I saw the psychiatrist, he ordered an antidepressant and antianxiety medication. I needed help, so I took the medication. However, it wasn't as easy to overcome the internal tapes blaring in my head about the stigma connected with taking such medications. That battle raged for months before a friend confronted me on this issue. "You are accepting when others need psychotropic medications. As a nurse, you've encouraged patients to seek the same help from their doctors. People who need medication for depression are just like people who need insulin for diabetes." Ouch. The truth hurt, and I had to work through the false pride remaining in my heart.[103]

During this emotionally challenging time, I brought my pain to the Lord, but I also focused outward as I prayed, *Lord give me a way to influence my neighborhood for you.* Conscious of my prayer, when I could sit outside on the front porch I would make an effort to talk with my neighbors. Weeks after moving in with two other women, my neighbor's mother came to the USA from Russia for an extended stay. She, too, was home all day caring for her grandson. My friendship with the toddler provided a natural way to connect. Babushka, as her grandson referred to her, and I had a problem—she spoke Russian and I didn't. In an attempt to communicate, we used a Russian/English dictionary. Through our limited understanding, I learned that she was a university professor in Russia.

While praying a few weeks after meeting Babushka, the Lord encouraged me to buy Josh McDowell's books *More than a Carpenter* and *Evidence that Demands a Verdict,* translated into Russian. When I gave them to Babushka, she had a smile on her face and through her daughter's translation she said, "It's my birthday today. I have always wanted to read about Christianity but never had the opportunity."

Not long afterward, Babushka returned home. I don't know how God used the books in her life. Nevertheless, he provided renewed energy through this incident and a needed boost of encouragement to keep obeying and praying. By the comfort of the Holy Spirit-ual Director, God's light shone into my "dark night of the soul," providing a grace-filled compass of hope, divine medicine.

When health permitted, hungry to learn more by listening to others pray, I would attend a weekly noontime prayer meeting. From January through April 1997, I house-sat in Glen Ellyn, Illinois, and began attending an Anglican church that met three blocks away.

By June 1, my health was stable enough for me to move into my own Chicago apartment, about three miles from West Suburban Hospital where I had last worked. As my health permitted, I continued commuting to the same church, now a thirty-minute drive away.

Then in July, I attended an all-day prayer seminar, a prerequisite to a twenty-six-week intensive prayer course that would start in September. Just thinking of spending the entire day learning about prayer created reservations around the "mystical ideas" that prayer really worked. What I didn't realize then is that whenever we pray audaciously—with boldness and courage—it will disrupt the complacency in our life.

The seminar lectures centered on building a five-section personal prayer journal including: (1) The Word, (2) Praises and Thanksgivings, (3) Intercession, (4) Petitions and Desires, and (5) Confessions. During the Word session, *Lectio Divina*, a Benedictine practice, was covered. Colledge and Walsh write, "After the twelfth century the practice of divine reading was often interpreted in terms of an ordered set of elements: *lectio* (reading), *meditatio* (meditating), *oratio* (praying), and *contemplatio* (contemplation)."[104] Evan Howard wrote, "At times *operatio* (action) would be included in the list . . . It is fair to summarize and to define *Lectio Divina* as a practice of Scripture reading which is distinguished from academic study, which includes elements like prayer and meditation, and which aims to bear fruit in the spiritual growth of the reader."[105]

Learning about this Benedictine practice created a stir of uneasiness as I wondered, *Does this method meet my doctrinal criteria?* However, in many ways the practice was similar to a nameless quiet time outline I had learned as a youth. In addition, as we practiced the method together, the speaker emphasized that we may make mistakes discerning what we hear from God, especially if we aren't in the habit of listening to him. However, they stressed that the Lord never contradicts his Word, so we can always test what we hear by Scripture.

I had begun learning to listen, but didn't dare name it as such, therefore I first had to confess my uneasiness to the Lord before I could begin practicing it in my quiet times. Yet I was aware that there are many dialogues vying for our mind and I was all too familiar with my negative interchanges. And I knew these discouraging thoughts weren't from the Lord, so I wanted to welcome "spiritual ear training" to discern the Lord's voice as a healthy alternative. By the end of the seminar, these new tools energized me.

As my prayer journey unfolded, I would learn that before I could listen or converse with others, the world, or myself by understanding the signs of the times I first needed to learn to listen and converse with my Creator.

Here is my September 2, 1998, journal entry, which illustrates how I incorporated *Lectio Divina*, albeit using different headings, and how this entry became part of my personal mission statement.

Devotional: In a prayer Foster writes, "May you now, by the power of the Holy Spirit, receive the spirit of prayer. May it become, in the name of Jesus Christ, the most precious occupation of your life."[106]

Scripture: Luke 13:12-13, "Yeshua called her and said to her, 'Lady, you have been set free from your weakness!' He put his hands on her, and at once she stood upright and began to glorify God."[107]

Communing with God: I wrote, "Through the occupation of prayer, being diligent, faithful, and obedient in this calling, may I grow my most precious relationship with you. I also wondered, *What would a prayer occupation look like? How would I ever know if prayer had become my number one occupation?*

Waiting Expectantly: While waiting quietly, I sensed the following from the Lord: "Alice, you are my child and I love you and will watch over you. Rest in my arms, and gaze into my eyes. As you experience my Fatherly love, compassion, and care, you will find rest and healing for your body, soul, mind, and spirit."

You may have the same reservations about *Lectio Divina* as I did. In an article titled, "*Lectio Divina* in the Evangelical Tradition," Evan Howard writes, "The 'divine exegete' is the Holy Spirit who teaches us the meaning of the text. *Lectio* is not so much about reading a book as about seeking Someone. It emphasizes the value of interior examination. And *lectio* demands response, the response of a life that embodies the values of the Word of God."[108]

Here are the ways a few scholars define prayer that also fit within the *Lectio Divina* model. *The Practice of Piety* includes a quote by Lewis Bayly: "*Reading* and *meditating* of the *Word of God* are the *Parents* of *Prayer.*"[109] Charles Hodge says, "We cannot make progress in holiness unless we devote much time to the reading, hearing, meditating upon the Word of God, which is the truth whereby we are sanctified. The more this truth is brought before the mind; the more we commune with it, entering into its import, applying it to our own case, appropriating its principles, appreciating its motives, rejoicing in its promises, trembling at its threatenings, rising by its influences from what is seen and temporal to what is unseen and eternal; the more we may expect to be transformed by the renewing of our mind so as to approve and love whatever is holy, just, and good."[110]

It took a couple months to put my prayer journal together so I'd be ready to use it regularly once the twenty-six-week prayer course began. Under the intercession area, I compiled a photo album and made a page for each individual and categories that included church, world, our nation, family, and missionaries. Under the petition section, I made a page for several categories, including relationships, body life, prayer and intercession, employment, personal change and growth, service, and more.

I was excited but nervous to attend the twenty-six-week healing prayer study because I wasn't sure if it would be too strenuous to attend once a week for three hours. The course was engaging and challenged me in many ways. The evening was broken into three segments, which included large-group worship (about fifty people), a teaching on a specific topic such as hope, self-hatred, sin, the cross, redemptive suffering, and more, and afterward meeting in an assigned small group.

On October 6, 1997, the third week of the twenty-six-week course, the topic was God with us and within us. During my small group, we were encouraged to identify idols in our lives or things that we allowed to identify us. After my leader prayed for me she said, "God is showing me a cluttered desk." Ouch! It was true but so hard to hear. By then I had lived with ME/CFS for five years, and I resented how this chronic, invisible, pain-filled illness had drained the life out of me. It consumed my energy, as I had to become my own detective, identifying what was causing my symptoms and then navigating endless limitations while making the most out of life.

Simultaneously, for several weeks during my private prayer time, while waiting expectantly, I kept getting a picture of a small candle lighting up a pitch-dark space filled with peace and order. *What did it symbolize?* I wondered.

These prayer scenarios provided a Holy Spirit-ual directional compass for my next action step. I wrote in the petition section— "taking an activity inventory of what consumes my time."

I began with housing—commuting twenty-five miles one way to Glen Ellyn where I went to church and had begun working part time in the fall. I had assumed I'd return to work in cardiac rehab near my Chicago apartment, but my physician wouldn't approve my return to nursing since this relapse had left me more debilitated than the initial bout. After that, my cousin offered me a job in their Glen Ellyn dental office. In addition, I was overseeing another cousin's empty house in Lisle, a suburb twenty miles from my apartment and seven miles from Glen Ellyn. While still paying rent on my apartment lease until June 1, 1998, I house-sat again between January and April of 1998. Indeed, *how long could I sustain such chaos?*

In April 1998, after the prayer study ended, I met with my pastor. He said, "I think God wants you to move out to Glen Ellyn." Relocating to Glen Ellyn would simplify my life, but for years I'd thought God wanted me to live and serve the poor in Chicago. While discerning God's direction, Scripture comforted me: "Without counsel plans fail, but with many advisers they succeed."[111] All my friends agreed it was the right decision.

When my lease ended, I moved to Glen Ellyn. While driving the rental truck to my new apartment, I sensed God's confirmation. *You will serve the poor in a bigger way from DuPage County than you would have from Chicago.* I thought, *What! When and how will it happen? Is this really an affirmation from the Lord or my vivid imagination on the loose?*

I know the concept of "hearing from the Lord" can unnerve some! Indeed, the idea unnerved me. Listening in prayer proved to be a dangerous endeavor, not so much in a mystical way but in that it required a radical obedience. I still get the listening part wrong at times but it is then I'm reminded of God's attribute of patience. It is exciting to experience prayer as a two-way relationship. Moreover, the idea that I'd serve him in a bigger way from DuPage County created a healthy dose of hope and suspense.

Personal Prayer: Abba Father, your ways are beyond my understanding. Through suffering, my relationship with you has grown stronger. Thank you for the compass of your Word and the instruction to test everything by Scripture. If it weren't for the body of Christ, the teaching of your Word, the prayers and the insight by others, I wouldn't have ever moved to DuPage County. I wait expectantly for how you plan to use me now for your Kingdom. I pray all of this in the wonderful name of Jesus. Amen.

QUESTIONS:

1. How do you keep track of your prayers?
2. How do you structure your prayer time?
3. If you've ever attended a class or course on prayer, recount something you learned.

13

Walking a Stretch in Silence and Solitude

Silence is not much preached today, so it is for prayer to preach it. If we do not listen we do not come to the truth. If we do not pray we do not even get as far as listening. The four things go together: silence, listening, prayer, truth.
—Hubert Van-Zeller

THROUGH PRAYER, THE CONCEPT of simplifying my life kept occurring. Thus, the move to my new Glen Ellyn apartment at the beginning of June 1998 was a strategic part of the plan—to live within a three-mile radius of home, work, church, and the College of DuPage (COD), an excellent community college. At the trailhead of another new life adventure, I planned to continue growing in my prayer life and fulfilling the continuing education requirements offered through COD for maintaining my professional certifications.

101

Nevertheless, God had other plans—preparing me for another extreme endurance section along my Masada snake-path prayer ascent. On July 18, 1998, during a Sabbath rest at the Morton Arboretum, a 1,700-acre museum of trees, I sensed the following:

Parts of Prayer from Chapter 12		
Lectio Divina	**Definition**	**Alice's Headings**
Lectio	Reading	Devotional
Mediatio	Meditating	Scripture
Oratio	Praying	Communing with God
Contemplato	Contemplation	Waiting Expectantly

Listen to the symphony in nature. I am creating and orchestrating a symphony of praise in your life, which requires planned rest periods at regular intervals to focus on me. Rest, obey, and trust me. My time of communion left an impression, leaving me curious as to how this would intersect my plan of taking five hours of coursework at COD beginning in the fall semester.

Again, the theme of rest came up and now into a slightly clearer focus during my prayer time on September 10, 1998. The following thought welled up in me while *Waiting Expectantly: Majesty birthed in the midst of solitude and silence then magnifies his glory. Alice, do you give me your prime time? Your life, Alice, a symphony of praise, requires rest periods of silence and solitude.*

One September Sunday, during church, this thought hit me: *I will send you out from the church into missions.* During a prayer time in the *Devotional* section, I jotted down the following quote: "MacDonald writes in *The Peasant Girl's Dreams*, 'One of the hardest demands on the obedience of faith is to do nothing. It is often so much easier to do something foolishly.'"[112] The Scripture verse I wrote out was, "For by Him all things were created . . . and for Him. . . . He is before all things, and in Him all things hold together."[113] During the *Communing with God* time I wrote, "Through ME/CFS I have learned how hard it is to constructively do nothing in faithful obedience. I fight to do something when I'm too ill to do it, before submitting the fight to God and asking him to help."

Then on September 23, when classes began, the reality struck me during prayer that my health wouldn't cooperate with my plans. Overwhelmed with grief, during the *Communing with God* portion I gave God a piece of my mind, and wrote, "Lord, I worked hard to get this certification and I want to keep it. If I can't fill these five hours a week with classes, then you better come up with a better idea!" In my heart, I wanted to prioritize my schedule, convinced that I knew what was best for me. My questioning and doubting didn't surprise God, nor did it change his mind. He still disagreed!

This prayer time that began as a huge disappointment ended with the following while *Waiting Expectantly: Solitude of vibrant plant life, beautifully clothed on the mountains and vales, blossoms, matures, and displays God's glory amid silence, solitude, and sunshine. Joy-filled freedom, a majestic sanctuary of praise rises from the place of soul restoration. Quiet your heart and soul so I can purge away all that hinders you. I call you by name to be my ambassador. I am making you to blossom as a beautiful flower. STOP, LOOK, AND LISTEN to your surroundings. I will continue to bless you, Alice.*

I wish I knew back in 1998 what I found almost two decades later, in 2016, while reading Robert Alter, a Hebrew Scholar's commentary on Psalm 98. David begins by saying, "O sing to the LORD a new song."[114] Alter captures the essence of this psalm for me when he writes, "Celebrating God's kingship, the perspective is global, for His reign extends over all the earth."[115] He goes on to write, "There is a concordance between the human orchestra—in all likelihood an actual orchestra accompanying the singing of this psalm—with lutes and rams' horns, and the orchestra of nature, both groups providing a grand fanfare for God the king. The thundering of the sea is a percussion section, joined by the clapping hands of the rivers, then the chorus of the mountains. This simple, compact poem

. . . is resonantly expressive: the Israelites chanting the poem's words of exaltation, to the accompaniment of musical instruments, are invited to imagine their musical rite as part of a cosmic performance."[116] How can we sing a new song with a global perspective to the Lord if we don't take time to stop, look, and listen?

The next day, September 24, 1998, my journal entry reads as follows:

Devotional: Here is a quote from Sandra Wilson: "Spending time with God in solitude, experiencing the reality of his presence, and cultivating inner quietness creates the condition in which we can hear him more clearly."[117]

Scripture: "Gracious is the Lord, and righteous; Yes, our God is compassionate. . . . Return to your rest, O my soul, For the Lord has dealt bountifully with you."[118]

Communing with God: "Lord, you have been awesomely good to me. I long to wait silently before you this morning."

Waiting Expectantly: I sensed God's still small voice saying, Alice, I want to continue giving you good things beyond what you could ever hope, imagine, or dream. Take the five hours you would have spent in fall class time each week and spend it in solitude with me.

What? Shocked, I wondered, *Could my spiritual prayer muscle really stretch that far or would it snap? What would I miss if I didn't accept the challenge?* The challenge terrified me! Somehow, I knew God wanted to instill in me what Andrew Murray writes, "Unless we are willing to pay the price, and sacrifice time and attention and what appear legitimate or necessary duties, for the sake of the heavenly gifts, we need not look for a large experience of the power of the heavenly world in our work. We must begin to believe that God, in the mystery of prayer, has entrusted us with a force that can move the Heavenly world, and can bring its power down to earth."[119] I bristled inside, WHAT!

How would spending five hours in silence and solitude do more for me than renewing my Exercise Specialist accreditation? I could only hope that one day Murray's words would resonate in my heart. "Time spent in prayer will yield more than that given to work. Prayer alone gives work its worth and its success. Prayer opens the way for God Himself to do His work in us and through us. Let our chief work as God's messengers be intercession; in it we secure the presence and power of God to go with us."[120] Alternatively, that the words Matthew Henry wrote were true: "The more sedate and composed our spirits are the better prepared they are for divine discoveries. All must be silent when he speaks."[121]

When beginning my season of silence and solitude, I first had to remind myself that it wasn't an act of opening my mind to nothing. I remembered the old saying, "An empty mind is the devil's playground," and "idle hands are the devil's workshop." How true! Jesus said, "When the unclean spirit goes out of a man, it passes through waterless places seeking rest, and not finding any, it says, 'I will return to my house from which I came.' And when it comes, it finds it swept and put in order. Then it goes and takes along seven other spirits more evil than itself, and they go in and live there; and the last state of that man becomes worse than the first. "[122] And Paul said, "Set your mind on the things above, not on the things that are on earth."[123]

I wish that when I received the silence and solitude challenge, I had already discovered this quote from Maclaren, which I'd find years later, to help direct me. "We need solitude and secrecy . . . and in that solitude what is to be our occupation? One word answers the question—communion. We are to be alone that we may more fully and thrillingly feel that we are with God. . . . Solitude is the mother country of the strong. 'I was left alone, and I saw this great vision.' We get hot and fevered, interested and absorbed, and we need solitude as a counterpoise."[124] I could relate! "The thought of being alone with God will be a joy—or a terror."[125] In addition, David says, "To You silence is praise, God, in Zion."[126]

I did different things during the time of silence and solitude. There were times I felt too sick to go out, so I lay by my sliding glass apartment door, looking out while clinging to my thirty-one-inch cross. At other times, I'd light a candle and sit quietly contemplating the mystery of light that God created. Many of the hours, I spent sitting by one of the lakes at the Morton Arboretum or hiking through the woods.

Silence created a space for questions that were troubling me to surface. One day a friend asked, "What are you looking to get from giving?" The question festered for a couple days. In preparation for my next slotted time of silence and solitude, I lay prostrate on my bedroom floor with my pen, journal, cross, Bible, and tissues nearby. I asked the Lord to examine and show me the intentions of my heart. With fear and trepidation, I humbly contemplated the words, *Alice, what are you looking to get from giving and serving others?*

My first reaction was quoting a familiar Scripture verse, "It is more blessed to give than to receive."[127] Just as fast, the words from Luke came to mind, "From everyone who has been given much, much will be required; and to whom they entrusted much, of him they will ask all the more."[128] I wrote, "I also give because I enjoy serving others!"

A floodgate of pent-up tears along with some stark admissions followed a long pause. I give to get love, acceptance, purpose, significance, and friendship. *Ouch! Really? I never knew it. Did those words really spill out of MY heart?* Acknowledging that my motives weren't all pure was painful. All I could do was cry out to God for forgiveness as I humbly confessed my selfish longings. As David Thomas writes, "All true authorities command us to commune with our own hearts to prove our own selves, and to see whether we are in the faith or not."[129]

God opened up messy closets during my set aside silence and solitude, when there was the necessary time for cleaning and addressing unhealthy issues. It was an essential part of the leadership development prep work for what God had planned—learning to live and serve in Christ, instead of serving for Christ. As Acts says, "In Him we live and exist."[130] Like most lifestyle changes, I fought against the idea of simplifying my life, afraid that if I limited myself to a singular focus—one of glorifying the Lord, I'd become so heavenly minded I'd be of no earthly good. I didn't want to become irrelevant or unable to relate to those around me.

However, over this season I began experiencing what Matthew Henry wrote. "In the service of God, and in communion with him, we have better employments and better enjoyments than we can have in the business and converse of the world."[131] Also, my friends would often say, "I can't go too long without talking to you or else I'll miss all the cool things God is doing in your life."

From that point forward I ask myself, *Alice what are you looking to get through giving?* before engaging in any new service opportunities. I adapted a practice I learned from my friend, Jen. Before making a decision, she would say, "First I must talk with my husband." As a single person, I modified her policy and instituted a twenty-four hour pause for prayer before responding. And it helped me begin identifying the unhealthy warning signs that required saying "no" graciously and without residual guilt, a vital part of learning to serve from a healthy place. These were important steps along my spiritual development path and for the plan God would begin to reveal in 2003.

Personal Prayer: Oh, Lord God, you indeed are the Great Physician. In silence and solitude, you excise the diseased growths in my soul. Thank you for the ongoing invitation to deepen my father-daughter relationship. I love you, Abba Father. Amen.

QUESTIONS:

1. Tell about a resource that helped shape your understanding of prayer.

2. Describe a practice that you incorporate into your prayer time.

3. What are your thoughts or experiences of being alone with God?

4. Have you ever stretched your silence and solitude muscle, and if so, how?

14

Acknowledging the Roots

Like the eagle soaring high above the storm, his trust in God towered above all immediate calamities and dangers, and his confidence was not misplaced.
—William Gardner Blaikie

THE ALL-DAY PRAYER seminar and the twenty-six-week prayer course had given me a thirst for more. I longed to continue growing in and soaring with the Lord. My next adventure was attending a weeklong international prayer school and later being a prayer minister for the school during the summers of 1998 through 2000.

On June 7, 1999, during the preconference Communion service, my pastor prayed, "Alice, I see the Lord's hand spanning and encompassing all of your life from here back to a yellow school bus." *Oh no! The yellow school bus! Nearly a quarter century ago!* He continued, "All the energy sapped and taken out of you before then would be healed and restored." Stunned, I wondered, *Who told him about the traumatic yellow school bus?*

Back in January 1976, during the second semester of eighth grade, federal law forced me to leave Arthur Junior High, a mile from home, and board the yellow school bus. Culture shock descended on me during that six-mile ride to Joy Junior High School (JJHS). The first week of school ended with only a fraction of the white students remaining, the result of "white flight."

Amid the volatile twenty-six weeks at JJHS, the movie *Roots*, based on Alex Haley's book, aired. Students and teachers, now fixated on getting back to their "roots," unleashed their anger and hate on the whites stepping off the yellow buses—adding insult to the injury of changing schools.

The federal mandate that attempted to make school a better place for all forced me to institute a personal survival plan. One tactic was hiding my intelligence by rarely studying, attending school twice a week (with my parents' permission), trying to become invisible, all while maintaining my 4.0 grade point average. I never dared venture into gym class, dubbed "Death Valley." Yes, it was part of my class schedule, and up until that semester was my favorite subject, but instead I took cover in Mrs. Smith's music room, practicing my violin.[132]

God had prepared the soil of my heart during the silence and solitude season I had just completed in the fall of 1998, and my pastor's prayer was part of the soul action that the Lord would cultivate throughout the conference. His prayer was a spiritual energy booster that provided strength during the week to identify gifts, talents, and skills that had been suppressed during the failed social busing experiment back in 1976.

On Friday, June 11, 1999, as the conference concluded, I was exhausted but exhilarated. I wasn't prepared for the last verses read from Jeremiah 1:4-9—the same ones I put on my short-term summer missionary prayer card for Zimbabwe, Africa, back in 1983. The Lord assures Jeremiah that he formed him, knew him, and appointed him a prophet. Then Jeremiah describes his fears, "'Ah, Lord GOD! Behold, I do not know how to speak, for I am only a young man.' But the LORD said to me, "Do not say, 'I am only a young man,' because everywhere I send you, you shall go, and whatever I command you, you shall speak. 'Do not be afraid of them or their hostile faces, for I am with you always to protect you *and* deliver you,' says the LORD."[133] *My voice!* It was a confirmation from God to reclaim my voice.

During the prayer finale, the sealing, and the commissioning, my pastor prayed again for me. "You will not do ministry by weighing the pros and cons of how much you can do, but by giving and receiving as the Lord continues to bring healing within your soul. A healthy balance of both giving and receiving." I left the conference with my spiritual tank full and the knowledge that the only way forward was one God-led action step at a time. Days later I wrote in my journal, "May I gird myself with your promises throughout this transformation process."

While still trying to break free from the devastation of my 1976 semester at JJHS, I remembered how fear had taken up residence in my soul. A deep-seated depression followed, snuffing out my once vibrant self. I, an extreme extrovert, quit talking, wishing to become invisible and thus preventing further bullying. To no avail! Instead, things got worse. There was the gooey gum someone put on my seat, hoping I wouldn't notice when I sat down—and I didn't! In graphics art class, there was the "friendly pat on my back," with a hand full of ink, leaving a huge ink stain on my brand-new blouse! At the end of another school day, students made a human barricade preventing me from getting to the school bus! What they didn't know was that my twin brother wouldn't allow the bus to pull away without me. The aftermath of those experiences was a gum-ruined pair of pants, an ink-stained blouse, and a devastated teenage ego.

Now, five months after the prayer conference, on November 3, 1999, I journaled what I sensed God instilling in my heart. "I have gifted you, Alice, in many ways. Don't be afraid to use your gifts . . . I orchestrate all things in my heavenly timing . . . Allow me to tear down the walls of fear behind which your giftedness hides."

This wasn't the first time I'd been made aware of how I had hidden my gifts and talents behind fear. It came up in the late 1980s when Dr. Dave McKay, my counselor, said, "Alice, you are like a designated hitter. You come up to bat, hit a home run, and as soon as the heads begin spinning you disappear, leaving the crowd wondering, 'who was that person? Where has she been all this time?' Then you're out of sight till your next appearance."

I began to address this issue in 1999, by volunteering alongside one of the pastors. This allowed the church leadership staff to get to know me and discover my strengths and talents. They matched my gifting with the needs within the church and asked me to be part of the benevolence committee. While working with three appointed committee members, we identified a need for someone to co-teach a financial course for the congregation. Here I was able to step into a strength of mine.

Also during this discovery period, again during prayer, I received a picture. I was wearing steel-plated armor that was too small. The armor had grown into my skin, which made the removal a delicate process. With each gifting the leadership team uncovered, I had to confront the fear that accompanied it.

The benevolence team also faced a situation that intersected with my professional home health nursing expertise. When they asked for my advice, I put together an extensive list of things that needed addressing. My list blindsided the benevolence team who didn't have the training to identify any of the issues. The lack of understanding about the situation between the team and me created confusion. The aftermath was awkward and painful, but with the gentle assistance from my teammates as they spoke truth into my life, they invited me to remove pieces of the obsolete armor I had clung to for protection.

Months later, in the spring of 2000, I made a trip to see my parents, who were still living in my childhood Detroit home. While visiting, I returned to JJHS to pray and put closure to that semester, twenty-four years earlier, where I needed the now outgrown armor to survive. Upon entering the office, I introduced myself and said, "I was a student here back in 1976. May I walk through the school?"

Permission granted, I exited the office and proceeded to the gym, where I ran a victory lap. Next I climbed a flight of steps to the second floor—déjà vu! The same chaotic noise ricocheted down the hallway from the same home economics classroom with the same teacher. As I concluded my visit, I recalled the festering prejudice that grew within my soul throughout that painful semester. I knew then that such a heart problem saddened God. Jesus said, "Love your neighbor as yourself."[134] And there I remembered the question I asked myself back then, *How will I find love for my classmates?*

When exiting the school for the last time, I recounted a familiar verse: "And we know that God causes all things to work together for good to those who love God, to those who are called according to His purpose."[135] I still didn't know all the ways God would redeem this difficult situation for his glory, but I prayed *God, let me take the best from JJHS and leave the rest behind.* And I would continue to trust and obey as each next step became clear.

The education JJHS provided wasn't academic but comprehensive, outfitting me with a needed global perspective, lessons that textbooks couldn't teach. For instance, it showed me how difficult life is for many, and it provided a heightened sensitivity to being a minority. The disparity between social classes opened my eyes, granted me a grateful heart for the resources I had, and helped me look with compassion on the poor and underserved. I also was able to see that even though the African American and Caucasian American cultures may "speak the same language," we have our own unique cultures. I also acknowledged the Lord's grace and mercy in allowing me to skip an entire semester without falling behind academically. It gave me a greater awareness that "from everyone who has been given much, much will be required."[136]

In hindsight, I could see how *Roots* created a lingering curiosity, which was the reason I spent nine weeks in Zimbabwe back during the summer of 1983. I was in search of the African "roots" of my classmates from JJHS. A delightful memory was living with my hosts, the Nyatsambos. Each of them shared their culture with me, each was interested in learning about mine, and included me in their daily routine; and there a lifelong friendship was born. While working for Scripture Union, Zimbabwe, the friendly social interactions with my Shona and Afrikaans colleagues were comforting. When speaking to elementary classes and at camp meetings, I was cognizant of being "the person of color," but this time experiencing a restorative acceptance.

I observed Zimbabweans caring for their loved ones and learning God's Word while visiting Karanda Mission Hospital and Chinhoyi Evangelical Bible College, two of TEAM's sites. Even though village life required hard work, without the amenities of a gas stove or running water, I admired that relationships came first, where there was always time for tea.

Zimbabwe was a significant chapter in my reconciliation journey. The healthy, accepting interactions facilitated a loving and safe place to acknowledge my prejudice, confess it to God, and move forward. "You will know the truth, and the truth will make you free."[137] My love for the Zimbabweans laid a healthy foundation from which to engage African Americans upon my return to the USA.

In June 2000, I attended the international prayer school again as a prayer minister. On Friday June 16, 2000, during the commissioning finale, a prayer minister said, "Clarify Alice's vision." The prayer was similar to something I recorded the same month. "Show me how my gifts can invite those in need into the transforming work of Christ. May I breathe out a hope to the world that you, Lord, have breathed into me."

Having shed the outgrown armor, I was now experiencing a verse from the Psalms: "He brought me out into a spacious place; he rescued me because he delighted in me."[138] This new unfamiliar spacious place left me searching for the old boundaries. I wondered, *What are the rules to this newfound spiritual freedom?*

Personal Prayer: Victorious Father, through your Word, through prayer and obedience, and through the words and actions of others I have experienced transformation. Thank you for the promise of Scripture that I will know the truth and the truth will set me free. (John 8:32) Lord, I desire to live my life for you. Give me the strength to do so. Thank you for allowing me the gift of walking in a spacious place, one where you delight in me. In the precious name of the Lamb, I pray, amen.

QUESTIONS:

1. Recount a prayer insight that you received from someone who prayed for you.
2. What is a Scripture verse that is special to you and why?
3. What has been a significant event in your spiritual journey and why?

15

From the Switchbacks— a New Perspective

You cannot be always torn in two. You will have to be one and whole
for many years. You have so much to enjoy and to be, and to do.
—J. R. R. Tolkien

A 2016 RADIO BROADCAST would years later give retrospective meaning to events that were yet to happen in 2001 to 2003. Before detailing the challenges that I encountered in 2001, the following interview summarizes perspectives and events that would only become clear when reflecting back on them.

I will begin with the question Frankie Picasso, host of *Mission Unstoppable,* asked without warning in a radio interview that took place on July 19, 2016. "Did you ever feel like killing yourself?" Was this one of those places where speech teachers would have recommended that I count to ten before answering? Would my answer have been any different? Instead, without a second thought I answered Frankie the same way I would today. "Oh yeah, sure!" What made me entertain the idea of suicide? The reality of living with a chronic invisible medical condition that still didn't have a consistent name, a known cause, or any treatment options felt hopeless. Life was a burden too heavy to bear, since ME/CFS had stolen the things I loved doing, left an extreme extrovert as myself isolated at home, and now it was even encroaching on my ability to remain independent. I couldn't see any light at the end of the dark tunnel, and I felt like a burden to those I loved. It didn't seem anyone understood the condition, and my emotions had distorted my ability to think rationally. So, in my depressive state I thought, *Maybe God needs me to take this matter into my own hands.*

In this isolated, desperate place, I didn't trust my heart. Instead, I trusted God's Word. A verse in Genesis addresses this topic by saying, "Whoever sheds man's blood, by man his blood shall be shed, for in the image of God He made man."[139] Even though my feelings screamed one thing, God's Word was clear that I wasn't to take someone's life, which included my own. And here is where I relied on prayer as written about by John Gill: "The true prayer is not a mere sentiment, nor an emotion, nor a form of words, however scriptural. It is an importunate appeal to heaven, not merely occasional and verbal, but habitual and spiritual; it is an all-pervading and ever-ruling state of soul."[140] Another verse, in 1 Corinthians, that made me realize I could not act on my thoughts was, "Or do you not know that your body is a temple of the Holy Spirit who is in you, whom you have from God, and that you are not your own?"[141] These two verses didn't take away the feeling of wanting my life to end. But in the darkness of suffering, with God's help and everything in my power, I hope to honor life forever.

Early in 2001, I faced another switchback on my path to freedom in Christ, disturbing the spacious place of inner contentment as I awoke to a third ME/CFS relapse. This one left me even more debilitated than the previous one, where now I could only manage intermittent clerical work.

As a nurse, I knew the word "syndrome" often translates into a garbage diagnosis. Worse yet, there is a divide within the healthcare industry over whether ME/CFS is a legitimate diagnosis or the "all-in-your-head syndrome." I thought, *If I had cancer, the doctors would treat me with respect. They'd follow a protocol that would end my symptoms, or cancer would end my life. But this . . .*

ME/CFS has demolished every institutional and societal infrastructure beam upon which my life was constructed. Instead, I've been left to redefine my life within an ameba type existence, unable to participate in normal cultural, institutional, and societal activities. Vidhima Shetty, staff writer of *The California* writes, "M.E./C.F.S. affects no less than one to two million people in the U.S. The term itself, myalgic encephalomyelitis, carries a provoking explanation: neuro inflammation of the brain and the spine. Individuals with the disease find the most effortless actions, such as walking, talking, or even concentrating, to be strenuous. Furthermore, due to cognitive impairment, they find it problematic to participate in any sort of lifestyle activity that requires even marginal amounts of comprehension."[142]

Prayer doesn't eliminate human emotions that accompany "one of the most devastating and overlooked diseases of modern times,"[143] with "some of the most underserved patients in all of medicine."[144] Where, as student Sophia Cuprill-Nilson said, "each patient is very delicate,"[145] prayer is not a magical suicide prevention measure. A strong faith and active prayer life, combined with the support of family and friends, a good healthcare team and treatment plan, provides the everyday and eternal perspective to keep walking forward under the Lord's guidance along life's switchback laden trail.

Here is how prayer helped me to navigate these strenuous Masada snake-path challenges.

One day in January of 2001, while home alone in my "main office" (lying in bed) I was having another "poor me prayer-pity-party." A teenage dream began replaying on the mega screen of my heart—wanting to do full-time Christian ministry. The Holy-Spiritual Director's light of clarity illumined the darkness as I contemplated, *Wait, what's stopping me from doing it now? My financial needs are covered through a long-term private disability insurance plan, (not the way I imagined, but they are being covered). My open schedule provides the time and space for my visionary tendencies to find full expression. I thrive on networking. I enjoy dynamic leadership challenges. I've looked for ways to participate in health care among the poor. I instituted the main ministry pillar of prayer more than a decade ago.* While in a holy place, God's grace catapulted me out of my "life isn't fair" drama and provided a divine alternative plan, a creative diversion to my chronic pain, suffering, and limitations.

My "work day" was just beginning as God highlighted my nursing experiences in a popcorn popping prayer way. (1) 1985–1988—worked at Children and Family Services adoption agency. (2) 1994—a friend's challenge "if God has gifted you to serve the poor, don't run from it but accept it as an important calling for your life," and (3) 1995—I attended an International Conference on Lay Health. I began volunteering in the Uptown neighborhood of Chicago, where in an eighteen-mile radius there were more than seventy-five different people groups and languages. (4) 1999—While trying to discern God's leading for ministry opportunities within the church, with the church's blessing, I began a monthly prayer walk where we would stop and intercede on behalf of the homeless at the places that they frequented.

On February 2, 2001, in the midst of my relapse I prayed, "Lord, give me strength, grace, mercy, and loving kindness to stay the course of following you as the fire gets hotter and the path more specific." Then on March 23, 2001, I wrote out this Proverb: "The spirit of a man can endure his sickness, but as for a broken spirit who can bear it?"[146] On July 5, 2001, I wrote, "Lord, my prayer dream is to begin a foundation to help the disabled pursue their dreams, hopes, and desires."

Even though God was changing my perspective, I still faced the daily discouragement from living with a life-altering condition. Yes, through prayer God illumined the darkness. One example: on Saturday afternoon, March 9, 2002, my Danish friend, Anette, and I were headed for an "American Experience"—High Tea at the American Girl Doll Store near Chicago's Magnificent Mile.

While traveling northbound on Michigan Avenue, we approached Wacker Drive, a busy intersection. Horns were blowing, brakes were screeching, buses were stopping, pedestrians were haling taxis, and every way we looked there was another car. It was then when Anette stated, "My clutch just broke!" Miraculously a clear spot opened for Anette to steer out of the middle lane to the right curb.

"Now what?" she asked. I suggested, "Let's pray." Anette replied, "You can pray, but I'm not able to right now." Silently I prayed, "God, direct us as to where we can go for help." Just then, I spotted a tow truck stopped in traffic around the corner on Wacker Drive. We ran to ask him for help. He gave us the dispatcher's number and ten minutes after Anette made the call, a tow truck arrived.

The clock was ticking. As Anette arranged the towing services, I became acutely aware of several emergency vehicles passing with their sirens blaring. *What is going on ahead of us? Will we get caught in traffic up ahead, or pass the accident scene?* In the midst of this inconvenience I questioned, *Why did this happen to us when our reservation leaves us only forty minutes to spare?*

After the tow truck left, we braved a fast seven-tenth of a mile walk with gusting winds blowing off Lake Michigan between fifty to sixty miles per hour swirling around Chicago's Magnificent Mile. While passing the gridlocked standstill traffic jam, we commented to each other, "What is going on?" Approaching Chicago Avenue, we got a glimpse of the disaster across the street where three cars were demolished. The *Chicago Tribune* headlines the next day, Sunday, March 10, written by Aamer Madhani and James Janega read, "Tragedy at the Hancock. Scaffolding falls amid high winds, killing 3 women; eight others injured."

At the speed we were driving north on Michigan Avenue we would have arrived at our parking destination, the John Hancock Parking Garage Structure, ten minutes after the clutch failed. Humbled, I realized our inconvenience was God's providential hand of protection from being a victim of the scaffold fatality. This verse from Isaiah became more personal afterward: "Do not fear, for I am with you; do not be dismayed, for I am your God. I will strengthen you and help you; I will uphold you with my righteous right hand."[147] It was another clear indicator that "My times are in Your hand,"[148] and this wasn't my time!

As I continued dreaming with God about divine opportunities amid my daily ME/CFS condition, by June 13, 2002, the idea for Sharing Shalom Ministries (SSM) began taking shape. The goal was to facilitate a creative outlet for the disabled to fulfill a dream, while enhancing their personal, professional, and spiritual growth.

In early 2003, only a few months after formulating my ideas for SSM, I was able to attend a free three-day professional conference in Chicago titled "The Nuts and Bolts of beginning a Health Care Not-for-Profit." Through a federal grant, the Christian Community Health Fellowship (CCHF) provided a comprehensive program complete with experts discussing grant writing, accounting, legal issues, and other organizational and incorporation procedures.

Lacking a platform from whence to do ministry, the dream of SSM never materialized. However, the process challenged me to develop a personal mission and vision statement, and I was able to pass along the conference knowledge with a friend who was beginning a Christian educational not-for-profit. Of course, not beginning SSM ushered in a slew of questions. *Wasn't SSM the way to repackage my disability saga into an audacious dream of full-time Christian ministry? If not, now what? How would God utilize the knowledge and resources I'd gained through the conference for his glory?* I did what God's Word says, "Commit your works to the Lord and your plans will be established."[149]

Instead, my plans kept crumbling with the next health-related switchback. On April 2, 2003, I read the following words: "Your long-term disability claim has been terminated as of February 14, 2003." My heart plummeted to a new depth.

Questions erupted from deep within. *How could they discontinue my benefits, guaranteed to me until I was sixty-five? I was only forty-one! Could God still care for me now that I was poor in spirit, health, and income?* Only making $450 a month working in my cousin's dental office, I was terrified. I cried, *God, if insurance isn't how you plan to provide for my needs, you'll have to figure out another way to care for me!*

No one had any answers, just empty words like, "I'm sorry and I'll pray for you." I believed in prayer, but at that juncture, the word sounded hollow. Nevertheless, I persisted, and on Good Friday, I wrote out the following verse: "Therefore, since we have been made right in God's sight by faith, we have peace with God because of what Jesus Christ our Lord has done for us."[150]

When I couldn't feel God's peace, I clung to his promise. I longed for a character-building confidence in Christ to emerge from my crisis, not an embittered fixation on my unjust circumstances. As I prayed, I acknowledged, "My insurance trial is not an accident but an appointment in your eternal plan, just as Jesus' death was an appointment in God's plan." I went on to journal, "While others look at my health and disability trials, may they ask the question, 'Who is her God?' I long for the answer to appear through my countenance as the glory of God radiates through my life."

A month after the insurance company deemed me no longer disabled, my three-year-old nephew, Ben, came into my bedroom in great distress. His shoulders slouched, and a frown covered his face. Cautiously, he moved toward my bed. With a trembling voice, Ben blurted out, "Aunt Alice, why are you always sick? When are you going to get better?"

I replied, "Ben, Aunt Alice's sickness is not going to make her die." A smile came across Ben's face. He jumped into my bed, gave me a big hug, and said, "I love you!" My nephew's words did more than any report could do to affirm that this condition wasn't all in my head."[151] Here was another confirmation that even when my circumstances seemed hopeless, my life mattered! In so many words, I had just made a promise—that regardless of how bad I felt, I wouldn't take my life.

The unsettling financial blow from the insurance company was a battle wherein I had to choose to allow the illumination of Christ to outshine the darkness of despair. Then, on July 11, 2003, God had another reminder waiting. It happened as I was barreling down I-94 at more than sixty miles per hour, heading eastbound toward Detroit, Michigan. With the gas pedal to the floor, enjoying the empty stretch of highway and gazing out at a serene twilight sky, I spotted two deer staring at me from approximately fifty yards. One deer and I were sharing the right lane while the other one was close by in the middle lane. *Do I stop, swerve, go forward*, were thoughts that raced through my mind. As Matthew Henry says, "Thoughts are words to him."[152] Go forward seemed to be the only option. With trepidation, I proceeded while wondering, *Is this my time?* I continued singing Awesome Beauty by Daphne Rademaker at the top of my lungs, "Lord of all creation we gladly bow to you,"[153] WHAM!

Shaken and jarred, I pulled onto the shoulder to assess the damage. As I exited the car, so did a woman, "an angel" from the car behind me. She said, "I wasn't sure what I'd find after seeing the deer hit the car and then leap over the vehicle and disappear into the forest." We both walked around the car. All we found was a shattered driver's side rearview mirror, and were baffled that the encasing was still intact.

After taking a few more deep breaths, I got into my car. As the "angel" closed my door she said, "I will drive alongside of you for several miles just to make sure everything is okay." After meeting my Creator in such a powerful way, I knew the answer to my question was in the words I had just sung, "Lord of all creation [I'll] gladly bow to you."[154] Continuing the remaining two hours of my drive, I understood in a new way that indeed God knows my every move and he will provide for my every need. Matthew Henry writes, "Praise is our rent, our tribute. We are unjust if we do not pay it . . . Thanksgiving is an essential part of prayer."[155]

Oh, and the mirror replacement was another example of God's provision. I bought a five-dollar mirror and then with my stained-glass art skills I cut the piece of glass to size and glued it into the casement.

Through prayer, God continued opening my eyes to see beyond my circumstances and to see that his provision began with protection. Trusting him through the switchbacks over the years was leadership training for the ministry position he would soon bring to light.

Personal Prayer: Oh, Mighty Fortress, thank you for the seen and unseen ways you have protected me. You have opened the eyes of my heart to see how you answer prayers. Thank you for keeping your promise of upholding me with your righteous right hand. In the victorious name of Jesus, amen!

QUESTIONS:

1. Which thought or story within this chapter resonated with you? And how?
2. Describe one of the ways God has affirmed you in hard times.

3. What Scripture verse reminds you of God's protection? Why is it special to you?

16

Pathway to Passion

When you have a dream that you can't let go of, trust your instincts and pursue it. But remember: Real dreams take work, they take patience, and sometimes they require you to dig down very deep. Be sure you're willing to do that.
—Harvey Mackay

BY FALL 2003, SIX months after plunging to the lowest valley of my eleven-year ME/CFS battle, I was still reeling from the termination of my private Long-Term Disability Insurance. It was here I relied on important practical things to sustain me. One was the encouragement and prayers of friends that came through e-mails like this one on September 1, 2003: "The verses I came upon seemed so appropriate for you right now, 'Blessed are those who trust in the LORD . . . . They are like trees planted along a riverbank, with roots that reach deep into the water. Such trees are not bothered by the heat or worried by long months of drought. Their leaves stay green, and they never stop producing fruit.'[156] Dear Alice, may you continue to feel the Lord's presence and know his peace as you walk through the deep waters. Don't forget to journal. He may give you important lessons to share with the rest of us."

The daily soul-care routine of prayer and journaling was vital for my overall well-being. The next day I wrote, "The magnitude of the loss of my disability situation is beyond my ability to articulate, comprehend, or imagine. My head pounds, I feel nauseated, my eyelids twitch involuntarily, and I'm using every last ounce of energy to make it through the day. During this difficult journey, I must focus on the known tasks and daily routines." Then on September 23, while waiting expectantly before the Lord, I got a picture. I was in the middle of the ocean, resting in Jesus' arms, while gazing upon his countenance of love, mercy, and compassion. Peaceful in the eye of the storm, when the hurricane struck, the winds destroyed everything that appeared secure, including docks, homes, and people, yet I was safe.

Another comforting gift was the hospitality of others, such as the spontaneous invitation from Walt and Ellen one September Sunday after church. "Would you join us for dinner today along with a missionary couple, John and Carolyn Lutembeka, from Tanzania?" Our dinner conversation created a spark of enthusiasm within. By the next day, God began encouraging me to invite the Lutembekas over for dinner.[157]

The daily prodding persisted, but I kept turning up the volume on my response, *God, I don't have anything to offer them.* My troubles consumed me! At such times, I was thankful for my close friends who spoke truth into my life. After one such conversation on October 24, I journaled, "Being a witness is a ministry of total transformation in God's presence, something done through me, whereas being an example requires me to do something. Through suffering, I'm a witness of God's faithfulness, which requires obedience, stewardship, and holiness." A long Masada snake-path route provides ample opportunity to nurture and integrate these virtues.

The following month I copied a devotional quote by Spurgeon, "The fittest condition of a believer is communion with Christ. It is not to be a privilege occasionally enjoyed, it should be the everyday life of the soul."[158]

Finally, on December 21, 2003, I invited the Lutembekas over. After a great meal and a moving time of prayer I asked, "How can our church help your ministry in Tanzania?" With only a moment's hesitation John replied, "If every family in the church gave a $100 gift, each gift would buy a new bike. A bicycle would allow a traveling evangelist to reach five villages. The distance between villages often requires a six-hour walk."

The Lutembekas had no idea of my love for cycling, but God knew. Could it be this meeting wasn't about what I had to give but what God needed them to tell me? I had to confess I'd never considered such an idea. As John continued talking, I remembered what I had sensed my part in missions was to be after returning from Zimbabwe back in 1983—to provide tools for national workers to help themselves. *Would God combine my passion and love for cycling into fulfilling a dream and allowing me to do mission work all at the same time?* I wondered. Here I thought about a Scripture verse, "Do not neglect to show hospitality to strangers, for by this some have entertained angels without knowing it."[159] The Lutembekas were God's messengers with a big vision for my life.

Ending the evening with prayer only opened a deluge of dreams. I thought, *Maybe I'll give the Lutembekas $200 to buy two bicycles.* Still only making $450 a month, I felt that was a lofty goal but I didn't have peace. God and I grappled for about three hours until I finally surrendered. I obeyed, giving $1,200, the amount of the road bike I bought back in 1992, when planning to lead coast-to-coast bicycle trips, the amount that kept going through my mind. Giving extravagantly required dipping into my savings account, my security net, and transferring ownership to God.

Within a week, God provided $1,500 back to me through three sources without anyone knowing what I had done. He didn't need my money, just my obedience and full submission. This sparked my next goal—to buy one hundred bicycles in my lifetime for national leaders throughout Africa.

Then in October 2004, I again gave away $1,200 to buy bicycles in Nigeria through a missionary. He bought five two-wheeled bicycles and five hand-pedaled three-wheeled bikes (trikes) built locally for those disabled by polio, landmines, etc. Without such a trike, those with these lower extremity conditions use blocks of wood as hand-shoes to walk, while dragging their legs behind in the dirt. When I received pictures back from Nigeria, I showed them to Bob Walker and my Bible study small group that met at his house. He challenged me to begin His Wheels International (HWI). Bob had prayed daily for me for more than a decade and reminded me of this every time he greeted me. Knowing his commitment of intercession on my behalf brought a greater level of respect to his counsel.

As HWI was coming into focus, I remembered the words my pastor spoke after praying for me back on October 6, 1997, "The picture God has given me is one where your life is like a top. The string is tightly wound up, but it isn't engaged yet." Unsure how to engage the string that night, I wrote out the following prayer: "God, will you give me an enjoyable position where I have variety in my work, utilizing my interests, talents, and education—one that would envelop my love for Christ into a God-sized position?"

Wow! Could bicycle transportation be the platform that SSM lacked for facilitating life transformation? Beginning in November of 2004, I committed to praying daily for HWI over the next six months and taking the action steps that God presented. On January 1, 2005, I wrote out my verse for the year: "He makes me as surefooted as a deer, enabling me to stand on mountain heights."[160] In response I prayed, "I cling to what you will do through me this year . . . Make my feet pliable to go to the high places with you."

Also in January 2005, having waited more than a year for a date, I had a Social Security disability insurance (SSDI) hearing. As the lawyer prepped me beforehand, he said, "I don't think we have a chance at winning any part of today's case, but we will try. Your work record shows that even with ME/CFS, you have lived at a high functioning level. That won't bode well for SSDI."

While tears fell, Grace, my friend and former nursing instructor comforted me, reminding me that God was in charge. Teary-eyed and trembling, I entered the courtroom. After the swearing in, I took a seat.

"Do you still have fainting spells, or was this a one-time occurrence?" the medical expert asked.

"I have them regularly. Often, when I stand up from a seated position, my heart beats so hard it feels as though it will beat out of my chest. I have come close to passing out on numerous occasions, but never have fainted."

The medical examiner thanked me, turned to the judge, and gave a medical diagnosis code. Subsequently, he gave a second diagnosis code in case SSDI rejected the first one.

The judge then said, "Based upon the testimony of the medical expert, the administrative law judge finds that the claimant has been under a disability. She is therefore entitled to disability insurance benefits."

After the closing comments, we left the courtroom. The lawyer was stunned. The medical examiner knew it and said to him, "You didn't think you had a chance with this case, did you?"

I received both financial and medical components of SSDI, with back pay for the past two years. God had gone before me into the courtroom.

Even though I had increased my workload to part time three months earlier, I realized my health could no longer sustain that amount of work. God already knew my health limitations. The medical component of SSDI went into effect the day my employment health insurance benefits expired. God's timing, again, was perfect. My fixed monthly SSDI check was $1,103. Given the amount, I was glad I had obeyed God in 1999, and paid off my home. In addition, since my SSDI checks were retroactive and I had not incurred any debt during that time, I was able to tithe $2,800 of my check to start HWI.

Then between February and March of 2005, I conducted four HWI exploration meetings at my home, where an eclectic group of ten individuals gathered to discern and pray. The group suggested we begin small and pick a target continent. A bike store owner in attendance said, "I have two used bikes at the store I'll donate, and I will give you a discount on the supplies needed to repair them."

In late March, while praying, I remembered Rise International, a ministry to educators in Angola, Africa, which I had heard about through Moody Radio. Once I located Rise's contact information, I called, since Africa was our target continent. While talking with the executive director she said, "We are shipping a container in early May from the Greater Chicagoland area and could take four bicycles." Afterward our newly formed team went off to work to find two more bikes and then fix all four.

In May, we formed a board of directors and incorporated as a federal IRS 501(c)(3) not-for-profit tax-exempt filing organization. Our mission was to mobilize God's work worldwide with bicycles (two-, three-, or four-wheeled). The idea was God-sized, but personal prayer habits had groomed me for utilizing the same needed discipline for my newfound leadership position.

By July, we had gotten the word out about HWI through radio broadcasts and two bicycle collections at a local church. Bikes were multiplying in my backyard, and I needed help. One Tuesday, while taking a Sabbath Rest, I was praying for a secretary when I heard a knock on my door. I debated whether I should interrupt my time with God and answer the door. I did!

The man at the door couldn't wait to ask, "Are you throwing the bike parts at your curb away?" Before I could say "yes," he was on to inquiring, "I see the bike rack on your car. Are you a cyclist?" I nodded and said, "I have just begun a bicycle ministry." After a quick exchange of information, I learned that Tom was a cyclist who had to retire early due to a disability. He said, "Six years ago I went to bicycle mechanic school. I'm wondering, "Could I come over once a week and fix bicycles in your backyard?" I thought I was praying for a secretary, but God knew what we needed.

It wasn't long before people passing by inquired about what was going on. Our team of volunteers grew. At this early stage, I agonized over what spiritual component to incorporate into the ministry. One day, infused with divine insight, I found myself sharing updates about the ministry and afterward I led in prayer. This was the beginning of our practice of stopping midway through each bicycle workday and giving HWI updates followed by group prayer, another carryover from the example of prayer the Zimbabwean leaders taught me back in 1983, and from my personal prayer commitment. As a team, we remained committed to pray and follow the Holy Spirit-ual Director's guidance.

Another opportunity that God brought my way was to attend a businesspersons brainstorming session on starting a ministry. I took pictures of the Nigerian trikes with me, and after showing them to a national leader, he stated the need for such a trike throughout Africa. I left with a new dream, *to take a welding class so I could build a trike.*

While pioneering an international mobility development organization, I was bombarded with questions from within and from without. Overwhelmed, I wondered, *Where would we find contacts? How will we publicize? Who will connect us to those we need to talk with since I don't have the strength to make cold calls?* Prayer for God-working opportunities, another personal habit carried over, was the only leadership answer since I didn't have the health to invest in pursuing formalized networking outlets.

Personal Prayer: I want to thank you sovereign Lord, for the Scriptures as my compass, for Jesus as my advocate, for the Holy Spirit as my guide and for the prayers and encouragement of others. Lord, I long to become like a tree planted along a riverbank, with roots reaching deep into the water, where I never stop producing fruit (Jeremiah 17:7-8). In the powerful name of Jesus, amen.

QUESTIONS:

1. What spiritual habits have you developed in your personal life that you have carried over into your professional life? What difference did it make?
2. What daily habits have you or would you rely on to help you through a devastating time?
3. How are you investing in personal soul-care?

17

Discoveries along the Path

Prayer is where the action is.
—John Wesley

THROUGH PERSONAL AND HWI team prayer, we experienced the mysterious, powerful action of prayer.

In 2005, a few short weeks after getting the dream to take a welding class so I could build a trike, a new volunteer was assisting us at a bicycle rally. As we talked he asked, "Would you come to my fiftieth birthday party next week?" Continuing, he verbalized the regret of not having any female friends. I attended with the hope of honoring and blessing him on his special day.

While celebrating and mingling at the party, as I told of my newest dream to build a trike, in walked a man who I didn't know but a friend of mine did. She said, "Talk with Kevin!" When I showed him the Nigerian trike pictures, I told him my dream. Kevin said, "I'm a mechanical engineer. Can I design, build, and pay for the trike prototype?" I was stunned! I couldn't wait to retell this spectacular story of God's faithfulness during our next bicycle workday prayer update time. Within a week, and only days after praying with the HWI team, Kevin had the first trike design concept on paper.

By September, just five months after beginning HWI, another new contact called, who I'll refer to as "Mr. (O)pportunity. "Could I stop by within the next hour for a quick visit, to discuss an idea I have about the trike?" I agreed and then scrambled to find two other friends to join me, since it wasn't part of my personal practice to have a stranger, and especially a man, alone in my house. As soon as we finished our introductions, Mr. O said, "If we partner together with the trike, we will get your product all over the world where our company has contracts." Four hours later at 11:30 p.m., Mr. O's Masada cable-car type proposal, quick and painless, hooked me. I was ready to move forward even though I never figured out what company he represented, their product line, and the international locations they serviced, or how HWI's trike would benefit all parties. And the prototype was still a design concept. My closing comment to Mr. O was, "I will get back to you within a couple days."

Sleep didn't happen that night, as flattering, intoxicating thoughts danced around in my head. *Here's our chance to get big quick. God won't mind this "Spiritual success"—right? My rationale continued, We could throw caution to the wind since we've prayed for such a spectacular opportunity. No need to worry; the unanswered questions will be sorted out in due time.*[161]

Wrong! Instead, the paved path of past prayers, from 2001 when considering SSM, was an invitation for the Holy Spirit-ual Director's guidance. Back then, I prayed, "help me not to be thrown off course and protect the ministry from those coming in with their own agenda." One thing this interaction taught me was that if we don't learn to pray and listen for the Lord's guidance in our personal time, then we are prey to the random advice of the counterfeit Mr. "O"s we meet along the way. The other important lesson I learned was that prayer must be my first stop, where I also ask, "What could we lose from such an opportunity?"

Ear training takes time and it is best to begin practicing in advance. The Old Testament illustrates this point when God spoke to Samuel about Saul a day before they met. "'About this time tomorrow I will send you a man from the land of Benjamin, and you shall anoint him to be prince over my people Israel.'"[162] Matthew Henry's commentary says, "*He told him, in his ear,* that is, privately, by a secret whisper to his mind, or perhaps by a still small voice . . . When God will manifest himself to a soul, he uncovers the ear."[163]

After the episode with Mr. O, I carried over the twenty-four hour pause, which provided an opportunity to seek counsel from the Lord and others before making a decision. My personal protection plan became an organizational standard. The next morning, I called Mr. O and said, "We will not be moving forward with your proposal!"

There's always a surplus of people ready to share their ideas of how God wants you to proceed. The reality is, if something is too good to be true it probably is! However, the thought of bypassing the organizational development growing pains was tempting. Prayer wasn't a shortcut, a way to leap from infancy, through childhood, adolescence, young adulthood, and right into being a "responsible seasoned adult organization" without the difficulties that come through maturation! If the HWI platform was going to be bicycle transportation facilitating life transformation, then the work first had to occur through my life as the leader before it could impact anyone within or beyond the organization. Even though there is always a Mr. O prowling around, there are no shortcuts to development work—personal, professional, spiritual, or international.

By late November, our first trike prototype (the lowrider) was complete. Now I wondered, *Where would we find someone to test the trike and provide feedback? How will we get the trike to those needing it in other countries?* As I prayed, God-working began happening through a thought, *Call Dawn Clark, the disability ministry director at College Church.*

During my phone introduction, I told her about our trike and asked, . "Would you know of someone who could try the trike and provide input?" She said, "No. But, I have another idea. Could you bring the trike by tomorrow and we can talk?"

The next day Kevin and I met with Dawn. We learned that her background includes being a physical therapist and having done mission work in Papua New Guinea. Dawn described her idea. "Next month, my husband and I are headed to North Africa to visit our son's family doing humanitarian work there. I'm wondering if I could take the trike plans to show Jeremy, who has been thinking of a way to serve the disabled. He will be coming back to Wheaton for a few months in 2006, and could meet with you folks. Jeremy has always wanted to learn how to weld and build things, and this may be a perfect opportunity." With the trike just completed and its first international debut now planned, we had yet another reminder that development work continues forward one prayer, and relationship connection, at a time.

Then in the spring of 2006, Jeremy and Kevin worked together on a prototype that would accommodate the terrain in North Africa. They did it! It worked! From 2006–2010, Jeremy and a team of four nationals built and distributed twenty HWI trikes.

Another God-working opportunity happened in early 2006. This time it was while talking with the Reverend Canon Habil (pronounced Ha-beel), an ordained Minister in the Anglican Church of Kenya. I came as a student, wanting to listen and learn as Habil provided advice on ways HWI could continue moving forward. The jewel he gave me came through a question he asked, "How is it that you don't have a prejudice bone in your body?"

Habil's question reminded me of the twenty-six years I spent doing personal work related to the difficult semester back at JJHS in 1976. I could never have imagined back then that JJHS was part of God's schoolroom curriculum, equipping and preparing me for Kingdom mobility development work. Matthew Henry writes,

"Those who undertake to speak to others of the things of God must have an insight into those things themselves."[164] How true!

His words affirmed what God whispered to me and I recorded in my prayer journal after visiting JJHS back in spring 2006: "Over the past twenty-six years you have worked through the test and trials of JJHS. From this day forward, those years will be the firm foundation of your obedience for the new focus and work I have for you to do. You will use the richness of this past experience for the present ministry needs."

Over the years, "God-working" opportunities kept coming as I crossed paths with people who would assist in the Kingdom goal of providing mobility through bikes and trikes to those on five continents.

One such connection came while visiting a bike store where I met Jan, a bicycle mechanic. She was instrumental in getting Naperville Presbyterian Church to partner with HWI and a ministry in New Orleans. Together we accomplished a mutual goal to get 150 bicycles to those impacted by Hurricane Katrina back in 2006–2007.

Then there was a missionary pediatrician and his family who received bikes in 2006, while home on furlough. When returning to Togo, West Africa, in 2007 the missionary called and said, "We are filling a container and are wondering if we can take the bikes we received from HWI back with us?" I said, "yes," and then asked, *"Would you be interested in taking a trike back too?"* After posing the question I went on to explain our trike goals: (1) To get one into different countries for people to try so we could gather feedback. (2) To find partners who might want to build them locally. He was interested, so off went another trike to yet another country.

An important part of God-working is engaging people and listening as they verbalize their dreams. One such dream, an important link in our ministry chain, came through our volunteer BJ, a member of my church who lived with Down syndrome. During our mechanic workdays, he helped by sorting parts, cleaning bikes, airing up tires using our powered compressor, and afterward rewarding himself by taking a ride on our trike. One day when his mother picked him up, BJ said to her, "Take the trike to the Joni and Friends (JNF) retreat!" JNF is an international disability not-for-profit organization with thirteen different ministry divisions. By taking the trikes to a Family Retreat, BJ's passion intersected HWI's vision, where individuals with a variety of disabilities experienced the thrill of riding, and we gathered information as part of our ongoing research and development.

Some things happened when I least expected them. One occurred on a blistering sleeting winter night in 2007. I thought, *Ugh I had better go cover the nearly 200 bikes in my backyard with tarps. How can I, a single woman with a chronic illness, continue running such a ministry?* I had expended the last ounce of energy putting on my boots, gloves, and jacket even before retrieving the tarps from my garage. Now out in the harsh elements, I cried, *Lord, help. I don't have the strength to cover these bikes.* Around the corner came two angels, a father and son team inquiring about bikes. "Can we help?" they asked when seeing what I was doing. "Yes!" I replied. After they covered all the bikes they disappeared, and I never knew who they were. It was an Ebenezer moment, "Thus far the Lord has helped us."[165] It was another loving reminder that God had chosen the right Founder of HWI, and my singlehood and disability were part of his perfect résumé.

Then there was the surprise discovery one summer day when my family was visiting from Detroit. "Who's here?" my brother asked as he opened my front room window and spotted a van parked in the drive. Since I didn't recognize the van and wasn't expecting anyone, I went out to investigate. In my garden, I found a volunteer who had already filled several buckets with weeds. My family got a front row seat, as they saw one of the amazing ways God provides for my needs.

By May 2009, when HWI celebrated four years of ministry, this was only a sampling of the many people God had brought along our path. We had already collaborated with thirty-one different US organizations, including churches, schools, etc. There was a God-working story lubricated by prayer, behind each of the 1,000 bicycles we had distributed, ten times more than my initial goal. We repaired most of the bikes in my backyard, before distributing them to international students, refugees, missionaries, ex-offenders, the homeless, etc. We had designed seventeen different trike prototypes (three different styles), completed our first production run of three sets of our trike's manufacturing process (four-piece fixture set), and an initial production run of three trikes. Whether it was the story of a volunteer helping or someone receiving a bike or trike, all were part of the growing Kingdom purpose of HWI, which was a by-product of prayer.

When gazing through the lens of God (net)working and responding to the heavenly nudges inside, I can say, *Prayer really works!* As I was transparent, sharing ministry and personal challenges during our workday update time, when we brought our cares to the foot of the cross, it provided a great equalizer, helping us stay honest, free of secrets. It was an invitation for team ownership and unity to grow as we carried the ministry burden together, depending on God for contacts, bikes, facilities, and finances. In the process, our individual prayer muscles grew and we matured in faith-stretching ways as an organization.

In my leadership role, I was learning that sustainable development work happens as an outgrowth of prayer, through the stirring of people's hearts. Each relationship God connects offers something needed along the snake-path of ministry. When challenged to begin HWI, I had no idea how my obedience would provide a creative Kingdom outlet for the talents and gifts of so many. Now I know the only way I want to continue doing ministry is through God-working appointments, lubricated by prayer, giving him all the honor and glory due his name. In God's economy, when he gives one person a dream, we know it is only one piece of his Kingdom- sized plan.

Personal Prayer: Sovereign Lord, you invented networking. Thank you for the gift of prayer, and the grease that lubes the God-working chain. I long to continue strengthening my leadership prayer muscle as I listen to and obey your still small voice, as Samuel did. And, like Samuel I say, "Ebenezer—thus far the Lord has helped me" (1 Samuel 7:12). Amen.

QUESTIONS:

1. Have you received a personal challenge that God used for Kingdom purposes?
2. Share something that has grown out of your prayers.
3. Describe how the Holy Spirit-ual director prevented you from making a bad decision.

18

Compass for Life and Ministry—Pray 10K

Man's mind, stretched by a new idea, never goes back to its original dimensions.
—Oliver Wendell Holmes

BY JUNE 2009, HWI had placed a production run of forty trikes through nearby contractors. I had more than 200 bicycles sprawled out on my property. In addition, ministry opportunities just kept coming, so there was no turning back now.

I was oblivious to the fact that people were watching the HWI activity swirling around my house, until June 4, 2009. As I trimmed my front yard bushes, a stranger walked up and said, "Excuse me." Startled, I turned toward him! He continued, "I'm just wondering what goes on here?" Being a commuter, he walked to and from the Metra train station every workday. With that I plunged into the HWI story while he listened intently, waiting for me to take a breath. Then he said, "I could tell something amazing was going on at this house. For the past six months, I've been trying to figure it out. I told my wife that whatever goes on there I already know I want to be a part of it." Our conversation continued for twenty minutes, which was the start of a new friendship.

His story was an answer to a prayer I wrote out in 2000: "Make my life one where, when people pass by, they stop and are forever changed by the gentle breeze of the Holy Spirit they encounter." I also wrote this quote, "Thomas Celana was to say of him (Francis Assisi), 'He made his whole body a tongue to preach the gospel.'"[166] I'm not sure how the Holy Spirit changed the commuter's life, but by his own admission, the work had begun more than six months earlier. His inquiry affirmed that my life was a "Reality Show," displaying the hope of Christ and not yet another American sitcom lacking substance.

Such an occurrence always humbles me, yet Scripture says, "In your hearts honor Christ the Lord as holy, always being prepared to make a defense to anyone who asks you for a reason for the hope that is in you."[167] The Lord used this affirmation to prepare me for the next Masada snake-path stretch, which would occur three months later.

Then in September, after reading the first chapter of Malcolm Gladwell's book *Outliers: The Story of Success*, I paused to pray. The words "prayer prodigy—10,000 hours" echoed in my heart and mind, spurred on by Gladwell's thesis: it takes 10,000 hours of practice to make a prodigy. By then I was comfortable praying one to two hours a day. In a state of shock, I wondered, *What did I just pray?*

Uh—hmm. With a need to know, I grabbed my calculator and began calculating the hours: 24 in a day, 168 in a week, 720 in a month, and 8,760 in a year. If I knew how to "pray without ceasing," I would almost reach my goal in a year. Since I couldn't grasp that concept, I began keeping a log, entering my time as I continued building my prayer muscle.[168]

In my mind, the timing of Pray 10K didn't seem ideal, as I balanced being an executive director within the context of my daily disability limitations. I wondered, *Could prayer be the highest calling for my life of limitations? Is my life of suffering with ME/CFS Christ's billboard, displaying God's glory into the darkness and hopelessness of this world?* Priscilla Shirer writes, "A life of obedience calls us to prepare for the adjustments God requires. If we don't prepare to modify our plans, we will end up more frustrated and overwhelmed."[169]

Days after receiving the Pray 10K challenge, I read a prayer of dedication for my new house, which I'd recorded in 1999: "May the King of Glory always be welcomed, worshipped, glorified, and uplifted, a lighthouse and place of hospitality where many stop by unannounced and are invited into a transforming relationship with the Lord." In addition, were two Bible verses I'd chosen: "For My house will be called a house of prayer for all the peoples."[170] And, "'I will fill this house with glory,' says the LORD of hosts . . . 'And in this place I will give peace,' declares the LORD of hosts"[171]

Jumping ahead another ten years, my 2009 journal entries confirmed this extreme prayer path.

February 6: "The God of our Lord Jesus Christ, the Father of glory, may give to you a spirit of wisdom and of revelation in the knowledge of Him."[172]

March 29: "It is not service that matters but intense spiritual reality, expecting Jesus Christ at every turn . . . If we are going to be ready for Jesus Christ, we have to stop being religious [that is, using religion as a higher kind of culture and] be spiritually real"[173] (Personalizing a quote from Oswald Chambers).

- April 9: "May only a vision of you satisfy the deepest longings in my soul."

- April 10: "I cannot give myself University training, I will to the limit of my power educate myself for His sake."[174] (Oswald Chambers)

- April 11: My prayer, "Strip away all that reeks of humanity. Wipe away all that hinders me. I wait with a holy expectation for you, sovereign God, to invade my every cell."

The Lord knew prayer was the non-negotiable leadership compass needed for moving HWI forward. In addition, singlehood and ME/CFS provide space and time, both hidden strengths for implementing such a redemptive, purpose-filled plan. Saint Paul wrote the following about the gifts of singlehood: "But I want you to be free from concern. One who is unmarried is concerned about the things of the Lord, how he may please the Lord; . . . but one who is married . . . his interests are divided. The woman who is unmarried, and the virgin, is concerned about the things of the Lord, that she may be holy both in body and spirit . . . undistracted devotion to the Lord."[175]

Of course, I never thought I'd remain single well into my fifties. Accepting my singlehood as a gift was a painful, arduous process. After working through the feeling of rejection as I wondered, *What's wrong with me?* I thought, *I want to be special, number one, in my husband's eyes.* After working through the "why me" questions that uncovered my attitude of entitlement, I came to the place of accepting that God's best for me was being single. *Nothing is wrong with me. I am special in God's eyes, and he has a unique calling for my life that lends itself to singleness.*

Prayer provides a framework, a rhythm for my unstructured days, a hub for HWI, and a focal point for evaluating, *Will this new opportunity add to my mission statement and Christ's call on my life?*

HWI has provided a platform for me to walk alongside others. Through bikes and trikes, we've encouraged the body of Christ by responding to the need for mobility locally, nationally, and internationally. I've shared my story through the airwaves, meeting the poor, the orphans, the prisoner, the disabled, etc.

What is the Pray 10K itinerary I will follow? In answering this question, I decided to use Herbert Lockyer's book *All the Prayers of the Bible,* along with Robert Murray M'Chenye's yearlong Bible Reading Calendar as guides.[176] M'Chenye writes, "Turn the Bible into prayer. Thus, if you are reading the 1st Psalm, spread the Bible on the chair before [you] and kneel, and pray, 'O Lord, give me the blessedness of this man' 'Let me not stand in the counsel of the ungodly,' etc. This is the best way of knowing the meaning of the Bible and learning to pray."[177] He goes on to write, "I fear many of you never read the whole Bible; and yet it is all equally Divine, 'All Scripture is given by inspiration of God, and is profitable for doctrine, for reproof, for correction, for instruction in righteousness: That the man of God may be perfect, [thoroughly furnished unto all good works' (2 Timothy 3:16-17 KJV).] If we pass over some parts of Scripture, we shall be incomplete Christians."[178]

By November 2009, we anticipated the completion of our second production run of forty trike part kits and we needed space. As I began Pray 10K, a volunteer told me how another ministry leader he knew had driven more than 3,000 miles throughout the county looking for free warehouse space. As I pondered the story, I calculated that he was aimlessly wandering for at least a hundred hours.

I decided that the best way for me to clock a hundred hours searching for space was in prayer, trusting the Lord to provide. Whenever I verbalized my Pray 10K dream and my plan to look for space, I did so with a sheepish tone, knowing the road ahead seemed ludicrous. Before long I wondered, *How will prayer help me find space?*

One day, in desperation, I went looking for property in an industrial park only three miles southeast of my home. I parked in front of a "For Rent" sign and prayed. "Lord, you know we need space." Afterward I remembered my property-finding plan, and went home to continue praying.

A week later, I took a friend who was in town for a visit to see the space. This time I wrote down the phone number. Once again, I had to return home and continue praying. Then, on October 31, four weeks after starting Pray 10K, while at a block party I began talking with a neighbor. I told him about HWI and our need for space.

"I'm a pilot," the neighbor said, "and I have space in my airplane hangar, about twenty-three miles west of here. You can use it for free."

I left the party elated. Here after seventy hours was another powerful prayer discovery, which I jotted down: "God is a loose cannon of creativity, which when directed by the winds of the Holy Spirit can provide a great adventure."

By late November, the day we moved our trike inventory into the hangar I had prayed 110 hours. Stunned and speechless, I was in awe of God's perfect timing. The space was climate-controlled so our trike inventory wouldn't rust, and it had a TV lounge, a refrigerator, a workshop, and a bathroom. It all seemed surreal.

On November 1, 2009, I recorded my hope as a prayer: "Make my life and HWI as a Holy Spirit floodlight, attracting swarms of people in the same way a floodlight attracts swarms of mosquitoes." Then on December 16, 2009, I wrote, "Help me not to do service for you, Lord, before my hands are consecrated and filled by you. May I proceed with your road map for ministry, not blindly setting out on the unknown road," service focused on prayer, not productivity. For my last journal entry on December 31, I wrote, "May my zeal and obedience to you, Lord Jesus, be such that provokes others to evaluate and implement such zeal in their own lives." A friend's words during this time were an answer to my prayers: "I'm amazed at how you have such a passion for HWI, yet you have the ability to hold it loosely."

Only months later as I was walking through Wheaton with my nephew, after someone greeted me he asked, "Who was that, Aunt Alice?" When I said, "I don't know," he continued, "Are you famous?" I paused to think of a polite way to respond before saying, "I don't think so, but I'm probably not the one to ask." He went on to tell me, "Yes you are, because every person you meet leaves an impression on their lives to the point where they never forget who you are." I accepted his insight, and through the innocent insights of a child, God mysteriously affirmed that the Holy Spirit was shining as a floodlight through my life.

One of the foundational pillars within my personal mission statement and as the leader of HWI is to spend my life on Christ— investing my time, soul, and energy praying with self-abandonment. Within months of starting Pray 10K, I had come to realize no one ever becomes a prayer prodigy but always remains a prayer apprentice. It is impossible to span the height, depth, breadth, or length of communion with the sovereign Lord.

Personal Prayer: God of all comfort (2 Corinthians 1:3), I thank you for the rhythm, focus, and direction prayer provides. The mysterious blessings and miracles displayed through answered prayers are awesome. Give me the strength to remain faithful for the journey of spending my life with you through prayer. In your wonderful name, Jesus! Amen.

QUESTIONS:

1. Tell of an observation that a neighbor has made about your life.
2. What are the spiritual rhythms of your day?

3. When has God used the words of another as an answer to your prayers?

19

Facing One's Fears

Our natural courage is as perfect cowardice . . . By the actings of faith,
we must fetch in grace and help from heaven to enable us to do that
which of ourselves we cannot do, in our Christian work and warfare.
—Matthew Henry

GETTING THE HANGAR STORAGE space in November
2009 was an answer to one prayer, but it created yet another
one—while this was a good intermediate step, we really needed our
own space. On December 5, this realization prompted this prayer,
"When considering the next steps for HWI, I realize I am a coward at
heart. Oh, Lord, would you lead the way forward, putting all the
pieces in place as you have always done." Afterward, God's
encouragement came through the above quote from Matthew Henry,
which addressed my angst and my need to rely on his sufficient

strength. He also reminded me of the ministry verse I had picked in 2004: "Have I not commanded you?

Be strong and courageous! Do not be terrified or dismayed (intimidated), for the LORD your God is with you wherever you go."[179] The way forward required radical obedience, courageously conquering fears and rejecting the mundane, to make space for the Lord's invitation to soar to extraordinary heights. Only he could take His Wheels forward in his way and through his miraculously orchestrated timing.

Pray 10K highlighted how spiritual growth was critical to leading such a unique ministry. Over the first six months of Pray 10K, I averaged sixty-two hours a month.

A question I often field is, "How can you pray for that amount of time?" Prayer is a relationship and each person approaches it differently. Emotional stresses that accompany a good, bad, easy, hard, healthy, or sick day affect my intimate communion. For instance, one moment I can pray with great faith, *Lord, provide the opportunities you have for HWI!* Minutes later I can battle temptation, wondering, *Is praying really the best use of my ministry time? Shouldn't I be taking action instead?* As the internal war rages, I am left thinking, *If I were to do something else for HWI, what would it be?*

During extended periods of feeling sick, my bedroom has become my "main office." Even when my disability makes me feel like a nonfunctioning member of society, prayer is an attitude of humility, surrender, and acknowledging that the Lord Jesus Christ is in control. Victorious prayer happens when I'm too weak for words but I consciously make a decision to relinquish, battling against the enemy's taunts to reject the Lord in bitter anger. In such a vulnerable posture of prayer, I experience Christ's words to Paul, "My grace is sufficient for you, for power is perfected in weakness."[180] Indeed a holy time can happen when my body aches with excruciating pain, head burrowed under the covers, and the future relief uncertain. Through a groaning prayer of ascent, reciting Christ's word from the cross, I exalt the Lord: "Father, if You are willing, remove this cup from Me; yet not My will, but Yours be done,"[181]

By April 1, 2010, Maundy Thursday, I felt challenged that month to increase my prayer time to one hundred hours, which was a huge personal leap of faith, at the cusp of HWI's largest hurdle.

A few short weeks shy of our fifth-year anniversary, April 21, we would sign a lease on our new headquarters, a 3,200-square-foot, two-story building, for $1,700 per month plus utilities. Scary, given that our promised monthly donations were under a hundred dollars, our 2009 contributions were $42,720, and we only had $15,000 in reserves.

On April 1, 2010, in preparation, I had planned to go and search College of DuPage's (COD's) foundation library database, a resource I knew about from a weeklong grant-writing course I had taken four years earlier, in 2006. However, I felt God prompting me to stay home and pray. After the first four hours, I journaled, "Prayer is the most powerful fund-raising tool available. Lord, show me the next step to take."

Prompted, after praying ten hours, I spent the entire Easter weekend in prayer. The next day, while praying, a man dropped off a bike. After talking for more than an hour, he later wrote, "Meeting you and then being awarded the extra bonus of chatting with you for such a long while was a blessing. You impress me as a quality individual, Alice, and I do not know many who wear that mantle well. I have met a number of posers but few who just naturally exude warmth, dignity, and intelligence . . . I was a student when talking with you. I learned from you, Alice, and am the better for it." His comments were a reminder that others can tell almost instantly if we are a showbiz or a prayer biz Christian. God used the encounter as an answer to two prayers. On August 1, 1999, "May I dance and sway as the trees of the forest by the gentle wind of your Spirit. As I do so, may my life provide a gentle breeze for those I encounter." And on November 8, 1999, "Make my life as the leaves freely falling on others with vibrant beauty."

The stranger experienced the light of Christ shining through me, one that comes when boldly following his promptings, gladly embracing divine interruptions, and then delighting in his awesome ways. After completing forty hours of prayer over the weekend, I wrote, "Doing God's work requires turning my insecurity and timidity over to him. George Mueller said he wouldn't ask anyone for money but he would pray, knowing God would provide. I stand in holy fear of this method because it seems impossible. Yet it is much more freeing to come before you in prayer than to go looking for funds." Mueller was a known prayer warrior for the five orphanages he began in Bristol, England, between 1836 and 1872. As he relied on prayer for provision, God entrusted more than 10,000 orphans into his care.

I also heard God whisper, "If you aren't willing to trust me and take a leap of faith by pursuing the rental property, then His Wheels will not grow any further." I know Scripture is clear about remaining debt free. One verse states, "Yours, O LORD, is the greatness and the power and the glory and the victory and the majesty, for all that is in the heavens and in the earth is yours . . . Both riches and honor come from you, and you rule over all."[182] I realized that my only option was to move forward in faith while trusting, obeying, and relying on him to cover our bills. He could provide all HWI's needs just as he had provided all of mine. If we were unable to meet our financial responsibilities, then we would have to terminate our lease. Knowing this was a possibility, our landlord granted our request to have such a clause written into our lease—no small miracle.

The way forward didn't make sense! But what were my options? If I caved in to my fears, I was committing the sin of omission. In referencing the life of Joshua, Spurgeon writes, "I would remind you that OBEDIENCE IS THE HIGHEST PRACTICAL COURAGE. . . . *Full obedience to the divine command involved innumerable difficulties*."[183] I could relate! The logical counsel from a friend was, "The style of ministry that Mueller practiced back then just won't work today. These are different days." Yet those who were part of my inner discernment circle all were in agreement with what Jen said, "Why wouldn't you proceed by faith? It is consistent with how you've lived most of your life, and God has blessed you."

I went on examining my heart. "If I believe God is calling us forward, am I willing to risk all for obedience?" I didn't want to live a life of safety, relying on my own security and forfeiting the blessings of obeying God's call, but a radical one dependent on prayer. I continued, "Lord, confirm your plans, show us as a Board how to proceed, and I will follow you."

On May 2, eleven days after signing the lease, I began another forty-hour weekend prayer time. I wrote, "My heart is paralyzed with a fear that only you can release me from. The difficulties I've faced in the past remind me of your provision back then, and I am trusting that you will see me through now. Uproot the financial fears that have been triggered by the decision we as a Board made in the light of communion with you. A familiar pattern of self-doubt occurred. *Have we done something wrong in going forth with the rental property?* Help me not to succumb to Satan's taunts." By spending time with the Lord, I could face the personal struggles before they became barricades to organizational growth. Scripture says, "You will seek me and find me, when you seek me with all your heart"[184] It is also a way to gain strength and discernment for a long Masada-like leadership snake-path. Unfortunately, on several occasions I've made the mistake of plowing ahead first with an impatient zeal, before stopping to pray.

On May 21, I grappled with a question impressed upon my heart. "Are you willing to go with me wherever I lead, even if you cannot see the way?" His question was an invitation for me to affirm a prayer from September 20, 1998, "May I be like a kite sent out into the world as a missionary whereby the cross is directing my course. Lead through the wind of the Holy Spirit and may I go willingly, allowing you to orchestrate the way." On May 21, 2010, my journal entry affirmed it: "I long to follow your dangerous and rewarding path even if it leads into uncharted heart territory . . . an invitation from you Lord, the lover of my soul."

The position of leadership and living out our dreams is a dangerous combination, which often sparks personal struggles that must be addressed. Financial fears were the obstacles that kept me from embracing HWI's headquarters, the fulfillment of a childhood dream of owning a bike shop. Harvey, our Jewish board member, dubbed it "a spiritual bike shop," a concept beyond my wildest expectations.

Months later I wrote, "Lord Jesus, when you were about to face total darkness from your Father, men were weak-kneed and unable to pray for you. I've felt all alone in what seems like an impossible HWI struggle, and a personal battle. You are here and you know the agony of an impossible situation." What I thought was the disappointment with other HWI team members was really the projection of my personal financial fears onto them. If I hadn't faced my issues before the throne, it could have surfaced as resentment to volunteers and others within HWI

I continued by writing, "You willingly chose to do the impossible for me, going to the cross. I'm so selfish I didn't think of your sacrifice for me in the midst of my own struggle. Forgive me, Lord. Thank you for being willing to go through the worst trial as a way of saving me and showing me firsthand the magnitude of your love."

By July 23, 2010, after five years of ministry, HWI had distributed 1,146 bicycles nationally, and provided 165 bicycles in fourteen African countries. We had fifty-three trikes on five continents, and designed fifteen hand-pedaled trike prototypes, which included two junior racers. In May of that year, we crated fifteen trike kits for Soddo Christian Hospital in Ethiopia, where a local would weld and paint the trikes. Then the hospital would distribute them. It was through God's answer to our prayers that the connections with more than fifty national organizations, churches, and schools occurred. Pray 10K was God's road map for leadership, complete with navigational instructions.

After logging what I thought were my first 700 hours of prayer between October 2009 and July 2010, the light bulb went off in my head. *This isn't the beginning of Pray 10K! It is just a redefinition, a challenge to increase the intensity of my journey that I began in May 1988.* By now, I had prayed more than 7,187 hours. I'm inviting you, the reader, to take the next step on your prayer journey and experience the words of the psalmist: "Come and see what God has done, how awesome his works in man's behalf!"[185]

Personal Prayer: Jehovah Jireh, I praise you for being my constant provider. Help me never to turn my back on the lesson of the cross. May the cross grow sweeter every day, knowing that obedience is the prerequisite for discovering your great mysteries along the path.

Continue your transformational work in each of us. I thank you, Jesus, for carrying the cross for me, a sinner in need of my precious Savior. Amen.

QUESTIONS:

1. Tell of a time when God was asking you to do something that didn't make sense.
2. What difficulties did you have to address before you could obey?
3. What fears keep you from actualizing one of your dreams?

20

The Rigid Road

People do not drift toward Holiness. Apart from grace-driven effort,
people do not gravitate toward godliness, prayer, obedience to Scripture,
faith, and delight in the Lord. We drift toward compromise and call it
tolerance; we drift toward disobedience and call it freedom; we drift
toward superstition and call it faith. We cherish the indiscipline of lost
self-control and call it relaxation; we slouch toward prayerlessness and
delude ourselves into thinking we have escaped legalism; we slide
toward godlessness and convince ourselves we have been liberated.
—D. A. Carson

WHEN INVITED TO SPEAK at Christian colleges, the professor asks me not only to talk about HWI but also to incorporate Pray 10K, emphasizing the importance of personal prayer as a leadership tool. As a result, students have asked, "Isn't it legalistic to log your prayer hours?"

In every area of our lives, we tend to evaluate things through the lens of legalism. For instance, I often hear someone say, "I made a commitment to do A, B, C and if X, Y, Z comes up I must honor the initial commitment." Legalism wins out even if the initial commitment isn't the best for a person. For example, when meeting on college campuses I've been shocked at how many sick students and faculty show up for a class or an extracurricular event. I've often thought, *It would have been better for all of us if you'd canceled your plans, stayed home, and kept your germs away from me.* They learned this by imitating parents, teachers, and even healthcare providers.

Legalism is prevalent in America's social values (or cultural gods), which include busyness, entertainment, money, power, and position. Many remain tied to a job or other commitments, which they have long outgrown, afraid of what will happen if they break the bonds. Yet we all struggle to place the Lord God Almighty on the throne of our life and then to keep him there.

Students bring up an important point when they ask me about legalism. I discovered that logging my hours as a prayer-measuring goal has positive and negative aspects. Let me compare it to the forty-eight-inch-measuring-stick requirement ("the 48") for rides at amusement parks. As a child, I dreaded seeing "the 48" near a ride. It plagued me even before boarding either the SS Columbia (1902) or the SS Ste. Claire (1910)[186] steamer ships, the connecting boats from Woodward Avenue in Detroit to Boblo Island. The fretting continued throughout the eighteen-mile, ninety-minute meandering boat ride to the Island near Amherstburg, Ontario. Angst overtook me at times as I anticipated standing up beside "the 48" to see if this was the year I could ride the Sky Streak roller coaster and other big kid rides.

The first time I looked up I couldn't see the number 48, and it would be several years before I was balancing on my tippy-toes. One year I was so close, but still too short. Defeated, my posture showed it—slumped shoulders, crossed brow, a frown that engulfed my face. Then I realized "the 48" had defeated me for the last time.

I could hardly wait for next year! The moment I heard we were going to Boblo Island, a shout of victory began, and when boarding the boat, I took a victory lap. *Today I will conquer "the 48!"*

It would be nice if the measuring sticks for success in all of life were straightforward like "the 48." Unfortunately, most of mine have been moving targets at best, causing me to grapple with the rigid road of doing-it-because-you-should legalism. Prayer is no exception!

The life story of Daniel is one that records his prayer plan, one we may call legalistic or insane when he persisted long after it became illegal. "Now when Daniel knew that the document was signed, he entered his house (now in his roof chamber he had windows open toward Jerusalem); and he continued kneeling on his knees three times a day, praying and giving thanks before his God, as he had been doing previously."[187] It was his loyalty, worshipping his God daily, which landed him in the Lion's Den. I wonder, *Did Daniel ever struggle with the feeling of legalism? Did he ever consider quitting? Did his friends accuse him of self-flagellation?*

By 2011, I had worked my way up to spending three hours a day in prayer. As I told my story, students and others would ask, "How can you spend three hours a day in prayer? What do you do?"

I had begun the year by adding Matthew Henry's one-volume condensed commentary as a prayer guide, though somewhat intimidating by its 1,986 pages and weighing six pounds. My goal wasn't speed but a Spirit led time. When starting, I had no idea how long it would take to cover the entire commentary, but I can tell you in retrospect that I completed my first trek in 2015.

The commentary came with high recommendations from Spurgeon: "You will find him to be glittering with metaphors, rich in analogies, overflowing with illustrations, super abundant in reflections . . . Every minister ought to read Matthew Henry entirely and carefully through once at least. You will acquire a vast store of sermons if you read with your note-book close at hand; and as for thoughts, they will swarm around you like twittering swallows around an old gable toward the close of autumn."[188]

A question that often comes when hearing that I'm using Scripture and a commentary as my guide is, "Isn't that Bible Study and not prayer?" There are many ways to read something—cramming, studying, memorizing, and/or praying through the journey.

I was in good company using Matthew Henry. "George Whitefield, God's lightning rod of revival on both sides of the Atlantic in the mid-eighteenth century, used to travel with his Bible, his Anglican Prayer Book, and the six volumes of Matthew Henry as his resources for ministry. He read Matthew Henry from cover to cover four times, and mostly on his knees."[189]

While trying to maintain my daily routine, I have made some unpleasant discoveries. Sometimes I approach prayer as a pouting child, unsatisfied because I want something else—a ball game, a party, a way to block out the issues surfacing. This has provided a gauge for showing me I still have a way to go in cultivating an appreciation for quietly meeting God. Just as he met Gideon during battle and said, "Surely I will be with you, and you shall defeat Midian,"[190] Matthew Henry says, "This divine person appeared here to Gideon . . . he found him, retired—all alone. God often manifests himself to his people when they are out of the noise and hurry of this world."[191] At other times, I allow the day to slip by having avoided prayer. When I evaluate the situation, it usually highlights a relationship strain stemming from anger, sin, or doubt.

Yet I know if I miss a day, my life temporarily ends up in disarray, having lost the centering that enables me to embrace life and not just tolerate it. Soon, a state of autopilot—rushing around in a blur, reduced to a robot programmed for accomplishing a list of tasks—replaces the peaceful state of God's presence. Maclaren writes, "The true way to refine and elevate and educate is to cultivate love to God. And when we get near to Him and hold by Him, and are continually occupied with Him; when our being is one continual aspiration after union with Him, and we experience the glow and rapture included in the simple word 'love,' then it cannot but be that we shall be like Him . . . Union with Him illuminates."[192]

An important follow-up step is confession, even though it's not a guarantee that the struggle will end. By acknowledging that prayer is a battle, it reminds me again to put on God's armor figuratively so I can stand "firm against the schemes of the devil."[193] David Thomas writes, "Christ was 'tempted like we are.' Adopting this view, we shall regard His spiritual conflict in the wilderness as a divine illustration of that warfare in which every earnest and good man is engaged; and there are four points of similarity:—It was a battle in the soul, a battle for dominion, a battle won by faith, and a battle resulting in glory."[194]

What's the solution to the rigid road of legalism? Balance, but without a challenge it isn't an issue. This side of heaven I will face that same struggle in all areas of my life, including prayer. Learning to balance prayer within a hectic life is worth fighting for along the Masada snake-path steps. I don't approach prayer properly all the time, but I have a forgiving God who is all about redemption—even when my feeble prayers prevail. Take heart; it includes your prayer journey too!

It's been interesting to see how my journey has influenced others. One such person was a HWI intern, doing his graduate degree in Christian Formation and Ministry from Wheaton College. Early on, he said, "I've never worked for an organization before that runs by the seat of their pants. I've always worked for organizations that have a (pause) five-year (long pause) plan." As he spoke, I could almost see the wheels in his brain spinning, and then he became quiet, his eyes got big, and after pondering his words, he continued, "No, I guess I've never worked for an organization that actually runs by faith alone. I have heard organizations speak of running by faith but I've never seen it firsthand or been involved, watching it unfold."

On another occasion, a professor within the same department brought a graduate class to HWI's headquarters. During his introduction, he told the class something like, "I've assisted and worked with hundreds of organizations, as part of a foundation, but

I've never seen an organization like HWI, where the Holy Spirit directs the ministry."

Even during healthcare visits, Pray 10K comes up. At one such appointment, the doctor asked, "What do you do for fun?" After hearing the same question a second or third time during a twenty-minute appointment, I cringed. I said, "My illness creates a challenge to doing fun things. I enjoy reading, going to the library, spending time with friends, eating out, and cycling some when my health permits." Laura Hillenbrand so eloquently describes the limitations of ME/CFS: "The physical experience of it is akin to being bound in plastic so that you can't move your arms and legs, you can't speak and be heard, you are suffocating, you can't see. It closes off the world to you in a most profound way so that all that is left of you is the thoughts in your mind because you just aren't capable of doing anything, of acting into the world or interacting with the world at all . . . That is the physical experience of it. You become a purely intellectual thing because you are no longer a physical creature at all."[195] As a result, I can't participate fully in things our culture highly values, such as relaxation, entertainment, indulgences, and sentimentalities. Pray 10K was God's answer to my prayer from September 17, 1998, "Help me redeem my unplanned schedule for heavenly value."

The doctor continued, "How do you structure your day?" I said, "One of the things I do is pray an hour or more each day." Immediately the doctor said, "Um, God, I need this. Oh Lord, I forgot, would you do this?" It was unnerving coming from a Christian practitioner. Yet later I wondered if the mocking reply came because he was spiritually uncomfortable.

Recording my hours has helped me reframe everyday activities into prayer. For instance, when hearing the daily news, I've become aware of the negative reaction it stirs in my heart. Afterward, the eyes of my heart began opening, helping me turn news into prayer. I approached it with compassion, mourning with those who've suffered, as Jesus modeled when he wept, displaying his gentle strength. Gradually I began viewing it through the lens of Jesus. "See to it that no one misleads you. For many will come in My name, saying, 'I am the Christ,' and will mislead many. You will be hearing of wars and rumors of wars. See that you are not frightened, for *those things* must take place . . . For nation will rise against nation, and kingdom against kingdom, and in various places there will be famines and earthquakes. But all these things are *merely* the beginning of birth pangs."[196]

Prayer has made me a participant in the gospel message, decreasing my need for being a seat holder at entertainment venues.

Personal Prayer: Father, in heaven, it is a joy to know you desire an intimate relationship with me, your daughter. Thank you for providing the example of Daniel who remained steadfast in prayer even after a law made it illegal. I long for the unwavering faith Daniel displayed to be a reality in my life. In Jesus' name, amen.

QUESTIONS:

1. What is an area of your life where you've faced legalism and how have you addressed it?
2. Describe a part of your prayer regimen.
3. Tell about a time that your prayers have influenced another person.

21

Fasting, Praying and Puzzling along the Path

Prayer takes the mind out of the narrowness of self-interest, and enables us to see the world in the mirror of the holy.
—Abraham Joshua Heschel

B Y JANUARY 1, 2012, we had been in our headquarters for twenty months. God had faithfully provided our $1,800 monthly rent even though it came with some nail-biting, faith-stretching times. The headquarters gave us a place for mechanics to work year-round, It also allowed for student internships, visits from university classes for leadership lectures or other projects, and workdays provided by youth groups. The space fulfilled my childhood dream of owning a bicycle shop and allowed HWI to continue exploring new ideas.

The downside of my dream was that running a building is a full-time endeavor where I found myself having to make many new decisions. As a way to explore further what was going on, I began 2012 by embarking on the next section of my Masada snake-like prayer path, instituting a thirty-day fast. Since my health couldn't sustain a food fast, I sensed I was to fast from initiating phone calls. I started by praying, "Lord, I bring this forty-year habit to you. Show me the ways it has enslaved me.

By tampering with my lifeline, I was left feeling like I was misbehaving when thinking of the unwritten rules that had me bound to a phone line. Days later, I received a call from a HWI team member that would begin the real test. He said, "I can't open the shop this morning." Since I couldn't either, I provided a couple of suggestions for how to proceed. After hanging up I felt guilty, as if somehow it was my job to scramble and pick up the pieces. It led to self-doubt. *What if I don't hold up my end of things? What will happen if I don't call?*

It continued past the present call. *Will the person think I'm mad at them? Will I get reprimanded for not calling?* These concerns highlighted the feelings of obligation, which fed my over-responsible beliefs. *It is my responsibility to keep relationships going.* My sin of using the phone as a way to control my emotions in personal and professional relationships was uncovered. A temptation I would continually need to ask the Lord to help me overcome.

All this from one phone call! Yikes! It felt like a huge ugly pit engulfed me, which made me long for a human to call and speak into my pain. Satan's temptations continued, "Go ahead, and call him back with the ideas that have just come to your mind. It's a quick call. It won't hurt anything. You don't want to create any miscommunication, do you?"

Instead, in this emotional, raw place I picked up God's Word and continued my reading in Isaiah 12: "Sing unto the LORD; for he hath done excellent things: this is known in all the earth. Cry out and shout, thou inhabitant of Zion: for great is the Holy One of Israel in the midst of thee."[197] Then I read these words from Matthew Henry, "Even God's frowns must not put us out of tune for praising him. By Jesus Christ, the Root of Jesse, the Divine anger against mankind was turned away; for *he is our peace.* Those whom God is reconciled to he comforts. God sometimes brings his people into a wilderness that there he may *speak comfortably to them.*"[198] Both the Scripture and the quote helped me put words to my emotions. *I felt lost in a wilderness and I needed God to speak comfortably to me.*

Satan had tried to avert my fast. However, by fiercely clinging to the cross and clothing myself in God's armor, I could see how Satan was using the same schemes on me that he used on Christ. It was his attempt to thwart my trust and obedience in God and to derail me, and then declare himself the winner. But it didn't work! Instead, the Lord won the victory and I was ushered into a quiet place.

I pondered, *Do I have the energy to keep maintaining our headquarters? Is this incident God's way of getting my attention to consider downsizing and refining our focus? If so, help us as a Board to discern what HWI does best.* Instead of depending on my own resolve, when instituting prayer and fasting as a leadership focus, God remained our leader. Furthermore, my disability was an asset that provided a constant reminder.

In the quiet, free from the telephone bondage, God began to clarify our vision, pointing out our strengths. (1) Consult, network, collaborate, and help others do what they do best in regard to trikes. (2) Provide our trike plans through an open-source model, as free downloads from our website. (3) Continue research and development, emphasizing proper ergonomic techniques. (4) Build a University Trike Consortium where faculty, students, and alumni can contribute their knowledge to improving the state of the art in trike mobility. (5) Create a trike community where others doing like work can communicate, exchange resources, and find help. Making such discoveries and getting pointed in the right direction was only possible through fasting, prayer, and divine wisdom.

As the month of fasting continued, I made some more observations. Next, I wondered, *Who'd ever tasked me with initiating all the phone calls?* This uncovered my belief that linked performance to acceptance and love. I also began studying the comments I heard from others like, "I hate talking on the phone; I have nothing to say; It's been a long time since you've called; etc." Another discovery was how burdensome it is to always initiate calls and how it cheats me out of seeing how much others care about me.

Then on January 23, in combination with the phone fast, I began a forty-hour weekend in prayer. While listening to a couple of sermons about Psalm 25 and meditating, I wrote, "Lord, help me to discern your voice."

During that time, I put together a 500-piece puzzle. It was the first puzzle I had worked on as an adult, but the timing was perfect. While slowly and methodically sorting pieces, I observed the different shapes, sizes, edges, colors, and shades. Some blended, making the similar characteristics difficult to differentiate, and others were mirror images, creating yet another issue. At times I needed to take a break, having lost perspective, unable to distinguish the slight variances in shade. Mixed in were a handful of easy pieces that fit together without a problem and encouraged me to keep going.

One day I began building the straight-edged frame; the next time I started from the inside to gain a different perspective. Upon completing it, I realized how the beginning of a puzzle is easy, the middle is harder, and placing the final pieces becomes laborious. They are the same pieces I've tried a hundred different places before, but once the puzzle is finished, each piece connected together creates a beautiful masterpiece.

The combo of fasting, praying, and puzzling offered leadership parallels and insights while re-evaluating our ministry focus. It clarified the dangers of fitting people into the wrong ministry positions and overlooking unique differences. It also made me consider how one lost piece ruins the beauty. And, if two different puzzles were accidentally mixed together, then what would happen?

A few years later, in the fall of 2016, during vacation, I spent twelve hours one day praying and puzzling. At times throughout the day I had to face the nagging anxiety rising from within precipitated by doubts, such as *Aren't you wasting your day away? Shouldn't you be doing ABC, or XYZ?* As I pressed through these external and internal silence disrupters I questioned, *When and why did I take on the role of being a productivity machine?* Spending the entire day doing a puzzle was new and different, but definitely not wrong.

Toward the end of the day, a person dropped in and said, "What an ideal vacation, to be able to build a puzzle overlooking the beauty of Lake Michigan. What I'd give for such a day." It was then I began to understand that the thought of an "ideal vacation day" isn't about time or place but about the state of one's soul. Creating space for quietness and receptivity before the Lord, and not being in an adversary place with others or oneself, requires discipline and intentionality.

These observations reminded me of how HWI's mission of bicycle transportation is also a vehicle for life transformation, inviting others to explore their dreams, visions, and passions. My piece of the puzzle is to help others find their place in God's master plan. Here I prayed, "I want to pass on the freedom and purpose I've found through spending time listening, following, and then obediently working out the results of my relationship with you." Jesus described it clearly, "I am the vine, you are the branches; he who abides in Me and I in him, he bears much fruit, for apart from Me you can do nothing."[199]

Up until that puzzling weekend in January 2012, the simple question stumped me, "How large is His Wheels International?"

Now—HWI is like a puzzle. A few people oversee the ministry, but the pieces, the people God is using to create the HWI masterpiece, are in the thousands.

Below is a sampling of the unique and colorful pieces of our puzzle we've connected over the first seven years.

One was the late Louise Troup, my mentor of more than thirty years, who became my "bouncer" as I talked through many leadership and organizational issues. Then in 2012, after talking about JJ, a prisoner whom Louise had corresponded with for more than twenty years, she encouraged me to write and invite him to be part of our team. JJ heads up Brothers Praying for Others (BPFO), where fifty plus men meet daily "inside the walls" to pray for us.

In one of my monthly notes with JJ, where I update him on prayer requests and answers, I wrote, "I trust all is well with your souls. The longer I live the more I'm convinced that if it is well with our souls nothing can sway our lives. It makes me think of the great hymn, *It Is Well with My Soul* by Horatio G. Spafford. *When peace, like a river, attendeth my way, When sorrows like sea billows roll; Whatever my lot, Thou hast taught me to say, It is well, . . . with my soul.*[200] I then typed out all six verses.

Three weeks later JJ wrote back: "I want to tell you something that just may bring a smile to your face. Yesterday a church member in Missouri sent me a few verses of this same great hymn. As I sang . . . I was wishing there was more. And lo behold the next day your letter arrives . . . the answer to my prayer . . . thank you for sharing the whole song with me. I now have and can sing this beautiful hymn . . . I am gonna sing this hymn each day and I have already fallen in love with it." As a way to continue encouraging JJ and BPFO, I sent them a hymnal. Through their beautiful part of the masterpiece, as HWI's prayer arm, God has also given them a way to travel the globe on their knees.

Another section of the puzzle came after receiving an e-mail from the late Jack Piers from Holland, Michigan. He had heard about me through a radio interview that *Chris Fabry Live* aired on   January

2, 2012. When he looked at our website, he found we were doing what We Build Hope, the organization he had just founded, planned to do. He wrote, "We need to meet . . . I am amazed at the way my prayers are answered. This is beyond even my wildest dreams, and I can dream some wild and crazy ones."

The next week Jack and one of his Board members drove to our headquarters. There we discussed design ideas and shared our resources. He offered to help with his tool and die company and the six-man team that was forming around trikes. Wasting no time, we sent him home with three sets of trike parts for them to weld and assemble.

Normally after such a meeting, I'd call a friend, sharing the excitement that seemed uncontainable. Nevertheless, my phone fast put a boundary in place that helped me protect this holy experience. Instead, I communicated my spiritual elation and basked in the victories God granted while belting out hymns and praise songs with my guitar. What freedom!

In the months to follow, Jack and his team would complete and deliver two trikes to Spring Arbor University (SAU), part of our Trike Consortium. SAU had friends who took one trike to a vocational technical school partner in Hyderabad, India. With the help of SAU business students and the India partnership, they built twenty trikes the following year and then were going to distribute them to those within a leprosy colony. The other trike went to a partner in Burundi serving widows. Working together allowed Jack to fulfill his organization's dream—even after learning he had stage four cancer.

Prayer is a heart posture before the Lord. If I hadn't obeyed and instituted a phone fast, I wouldn't have uncovered and then confessed some of the sins that disrupt my intimacy with Christ. Nor would I have gotten a clear picture of how HWI, and my leadership story of helping others complete one of their puzzles, attracts people who are trying to identify their dreams. We've also received the privilege of walking alongside others as their dreams come to fruition.

Personal Prayer: Father, how can I say thank you for using my life as puzzle piece within your master plan? May I continue to allow you to mold my life! Help me to keep an open hand for what you want to do in and through the ministry of HWI and me. I place my life in the Master's hands. Amen.

QUESTIONS:

1. What type of fast have you tried?
2. What did you learn through your fast?
3. What creative activity have you done while praying, and what discoveries did you make?

22

A Twist in the Trail

If I make God my Refuge, I shall get something a great deal better than escape from outward sorrow—namely, an amulet which will turn the outward sorrow into joy. The bitter water will still be given me to drink, but it will be filtered water, out of which God will strain all the poison, though He leaves plenty of the bitterness in it; for bitterness is a tonic.

—Alexander Maclaren

NOW INTO FEBRUARY 2012, after completing my thirty-day phone fast, I continued contemplating HWI's next steps. One day during prayer I found myself increasingly agitated by all the details related to keeping the headquarters going. I realized they were draining my energy, threatening my physical health, and stealing my joy. In that place, I came upon these words in Matthew Henry's Commentary, "We have liberty to open our minds freely to God, as to a Father. We may come with humble boldness to hear from him good words and comfortable."[201]

Since I'm not a person to make hasty decisions, the process, "What do we do about the headquarters?" continued. In the middle of June, while consulting with one of our HWI friends I said, "We are going to close down our headquarters and I'm going back home." After some discussion, he said, "I don't think it's time. I'm going to cover your rent (by then it was $1,900 per month) for the next ten months while you figure out what God wants you to do." After leaving the meeting, I felt like crying. I was ready to quit and go home, unable to see a way forward juggling my health and a building. But God . . .

The advice I kept hearing was, "You've got to think bigger and formulate a larger goal." I remembered a prayer picture back in 2000 that the Lord gave my friend Anette for me. "I see countless lights shining everywhere, off the points of a star." Through HWI, God answered that prayer, surpassing my goal of distributing one hundred bicycles fourteen times over.

When assessing how we were using our space, I couldn't get past the realization that we were paying to house about 200 bicycles—most of them disposable and beyond repair. Our trike work took up a very tiny amount of space, and it was the unique part of HWI. We had tried to have evening workdays and basic bicycle repair training to draw student help, and even made the space hangout-friendly with donated pool, foosball, and ping-pong tables. But it didn't happen. I also knew it wasn't good stewardship to use the space only two mornings a week even though we had tried many ways to expand our hours. Bigger was not proving to be better, but burdensome, as it was leaving me less effective. But God wasn't finished with us yet.

In the fall of 2012, while meeting with another one of HWI's friends, I recounted the most recent "God-workings." I assured the friend that once again, it was God's ministry and he was in charge. I said, "By the end of November I will have completed my Pray 10K goal." He said, "Maybe you should shoot for 100,000 hours. You can't stop now. We need your prayers." I thought, *What did he say? Isn't this the same guy who years earlier told me, "Mueller's method of fund-raising wouldn't work today?" Now he's presenting me with a prayer goal that I fear to attempt?*

It's true, there's no turning back on prayer. On December 1, 2012, I began my second Pray 10K, hoping to finish in nine years as opposed to the twenty-four years it took for the first one. I've made a plan to continue repeated Pray 10K journeys toward 100K. Nevertheless, I still wonder, *How will I do it?*

While pondering, *How will I accomplish the next Pray 10K in nine years?* I thought about my Carlton Elementary School days. The memory was that of hearing the school bell ring every weekday, morning and afternoon, for seven years. Pray 10K was a different assignment; however, the implications were the same. *It's time to prepare for the day's lessons.*

The 8:00 a.m. elementary school bell was just training grounds for a screeching alarm of another kind that sounded recently at 2:30 a.m. This one unnerved and angered every sinew in my body. Chronic pain stole yet another night of sleep from my ME/CFS war-weary body. Wide awake, dead tired, and in excruciating physical pain, agony drove me to admit my powerlessness. I cried the same words of David and of Christ, "Into Your hand I commit my spirit,"[202] acknowledging that physical limitations are the catalyst for eternal opportunities, for God-working, and for prayer in its rawest form.

I rarely respond to the Suffering Maestro's difficult lessons with such acceptance. More often, I succumb to the devil's taunting and engaging doubt. *Why me? Why must I suffer? What have I done wrong? When will it end?* This time, resisting the devil caused him to flee and ushered in a two-hour time of worship, praise, surrender, and remembrance, a soul-balm.

During that session, I contemplated how the thorn in my flesh, ME/CFS, the suffering Maestro's teaching, and Pray 10K were my encouraging companions. The lessons often followed deliberation over the agonizing consequences of my limitations: *Should I call and cancel once again? What will my friends or family think if I do? Maybe I'll be well enough to participate! Am I just being lazy? What's wrong with me? Why do I have to miss all the fun? My health has stolen my life from me! What can I offer as a participating member of my family, friends, and church or within society? My weakness embarrasses me!*

If we accept it, suffering is a gifted teacher. I pray that my life will be my best sermon. Broadus writes, "What is there good that cometh not out of suffering? And what is there great that cometh not out of self-denial? What is there new, in knowledge or in virtue, that cometh not out of solitary thought? And what is there noble and lasting in purpose that cometh not out of long nursing and strengthening in the secret chambers of the mind?"[203]

The benefit of making prayer my number one occupation is that it continues providing a compass, a daily rhythm for living intentionally. It also provides a place for me to scrutinize opportunities as I ask myself, *Does this opportunity help me best fulfill my God given purpose?*

Another thing that's come from sharing about Pray 10K is that it has given me an opportunity to dialogue with others as they state their skeptical questions, theories, and thoughts. "Do you pray and then God provides? How does prayer work? Who am I, to pray specific prayers to the Creator? Does God answer all your prayers in just the way you ask him? How do you know when he's answered your prayers? How long are you supposed to pray for the same thing? Are you really certain that prayer works?"

These thoughts led me to examine them through the lens of Scripture, with the title header of "Prayer and the Golden Rule: 'Ask, and it will be given to you; seek, and you will find; knock, and it will be opened to you. For everyone who asks receives, and he who seeks finds, and to him who knocks it will be opened.'"[204] David Thomas expounds on these verses, "Here are three words expressive of three different acts used to designate true prayer. The one idea conveyed by the whole seems to be, *earnest application to God*. True prayer is not a mere sentiment, nor an emotion, nor a form of words, however scriptural . . . it is an all-pervading and ever-ruling state of soul."[205]

As I embrace the Suffering Maestro's magnanimous life lessons, allowing them to permeate my soul, it ushers in a sweet communion. It also helps me adjust my thoughts and accept that God's plans are best. When doing so, I've experienced a foretaste of heaven and of Christ being formed in me as I accept countless prayer invitations—the eternal opportunities I've been given. Matthew Henry writes, "What God denies them he will give the grace to be content without and then they do not want it . . . Paul had all and abounded, because he was content."[206]

While thinking over my many prayer invitations, one that came to mind was the day I asked a friend, "What type of political service project could I do? I'm not very politically savvy." My friend suggested, "Pray for those in office." Paul wrote, "I urge that entreaties and prayers, petitions and thanksgivings, be made on behalf of all men, for kings and all who are in authority"[207] Ugh! I wondered, *How can I do this without losing interest when articulating sweeping generalized prayers?* There I had a "Ya-ha-weh!" moment. *Pick a military family and a person in government to pray for regularly.* By personalizing the process, I was able to write an encouraging handwritten note when my local politician was facing a tumultuous time. Afterward, I received an encouraging in-person thank you. In addition, when my solider deployed, I was able to put action to my prayers, through e-mails and a care package. Upon his return home from war, as he told how an improvised explosive device (IED) detonated a split second too late, sparing his life and vehicle, I could rejoice in answered prayers. During another season, I participated in a weekly political candidate prayer meeting. I grew in how to pray for those in politics as the candidate shared requests and I listened to those participating in the candidate's weekly prayer time. In addition, I was fulfilling my mission statement of covering new territory, obeying Scripture and at the same time encouraging others through prayer.

On my quest to prayer for the world, I bought the book, *Operation World: The Definitive Prayer Guide to Every Nation.*[208] However, before long I put it on the shelf, intimidated by the 1,000 pages and the vast amount of material it covered. I couldn't figure out how to break it down into bite-size chunks, or where to begin. Until the idea came, *Begin with the countries where HWI has sent trikes to this year.* The God-thought sparked my interest and provided a realistic way to incorporate this resource in an exciting way into my prayer time. Next, I plan to look at all twenty countries where we have sent trikes. I would echo an endorsement of this book by Dr. K. P. Yohannan, International Director of Gospel for Asia: "Here is your bridge to walk into every continent, nation, community and touch them with your prayers and commitment."[209]

Next, this reminded me that God would answer my cry about another missed opportunity. ME/CFS haunted my broken heart and kept me from going and comforting those closest to me as they buried their loved ones! Loneliness was deafening when grief pierced me amid the mix of raw emotions while all alone at home. *Lord, why can't I walk alongside of those I love in their time of need?*

In my sorrow, a holy revelation hit me. *Pray during the visitation and funeral service. Then write a letter to your grieving loved ones. WOW! What a way to participate from afar,* I thought.

I prayed, *Lord, I do not want my grief to stick out as an ugly thorn in a beautiful garden.* In the schoolroom of lament, while hunkered down in the presence of the "God of all Comfort," I opened the textbook of grief. There the Almighty Artist highlighted Christ's crucifixion on my heart's new landscape. In this holy time, I found closure, as I brought my grief to my soul Comforter.

During the funeral service, I explored the following Scripture, so diametrically opposed to our thrills-driven, twenty-first-century culture: "The day of one's death is better than the day of one's birth. It is better to go to a house of mourning than to go to a house of feasting, because that is the end of every man, and the living takes it to heart. Sorrow is better than laughter, for when a face is sad a heart may be happy. The mind of the wise is in the house of mourning, while the mind of fools is in the house of pleasure."[210]

In the follow-up letter, I wrote, "I pray that new life would come out of the death of your loved one. The thief alters the landscape of our lives, but lament is an invitation to experience a deeper intimacy with Jesus Christ. I have spent the day at the foot of the cross on behalf of your family. May death teach us the rhythm of our Father's heart. I pray these thoughts would encourage and provide hope to your hearts as they have mine." Over the years, I've repeated this end-of-life prayer care several times.

Here's another glimpse into the magnitude of God-workings and the mysterious measures my Creative Father goes to in answering my undercover (lying in bed) prayers. Upon hearing a familiar name over the airwaves a couple years later, my curiosity was piqued. I searched the Internet for this blast from the past—Detroit Michigan in the 1970s. What I discovered was stunning! In an alumni magazine, two excellent book reviews had highlighted different angles of the same specialty. One of the angles was by a university professor I had prayed for regularly over the last two decades. A disciple of my dad's four decades earlier wrote the other one. Only the sovereign Lord of the Universe could allow my dad and me to do ministry together yet remotely through God (net) working, while building the breadth of my prayer understanding.

Whether with the health to fulfill my flyaway dreams or tormented by grave troubles, the cry of my heart remains, *Lord, I long to live a life where I magnify your name when recounting each of my days.*

Personal Prayer: God of all comfort, I'm thankful that you are my Masada, my Mighty Fortress, where I can find refuge from suffering. It's my heart's desire, to magnify your name every day. Whether you choose to answer this prayer through sickness or health, help me remain an ever-faithful conduit of your Shekinah Glory. In the sovereign name of Jesus, amen.

QUESTIONS:

1.   Recount a God-working story.
2.   What is one experience that has deepened your prayer life?
3.   How have you responded to suffering?
4.   What has suffering taught you?

23

Learning from a Fellow Traveler

Nothing is more needed among preachers [leaders] today than that we should have the courage to shake ourselves free from the thousand and one trivialities in which we are asked to waste our time and strength, and resolutely return to the apostolic ideal which made necessary the office of the diaconate. We must resolve that we will continue steadfastly in prayer, and in the ministry of the Word.
—G. Campbell Morgan

WHEN IT CAME TIME to resume paying HWI rent in May 2013, we downsized to one floor, half the space and cost. We had a contract worker, a bicycle mechanic who we had brought on in 2011 for about forty hours a month to help us determine if selling bicycles was a way to support and expand our trike ministry. By the fall of 2013, we had run a few successful bike sale days and had gathered the research needed to make an informed decision. Yes, we were successful at selling bicycles. But, to sustain this plan would mean increasing our manpower and bringing in more inventory, which would further deplete my energy output even before addressing ministry issues.

Since HWI's finances, resources, and networking were God's department, we scrutinized our goals and prayed for wisdom to remain faithful to the Holy Spirit's direction, to our mission, to our board, and to our volunteers. Our goal wasn't numbers or size but receiving the blessings that accompany individual and organizational obedience. We never wanted trivialities to trump the Holy Spirit's leading.

Throughout the process people just kept saying, "Go look for funds." However, I heeded God's whisper, "If you go looking for funds, I will not continue blessing HWI." Okay! Now what were my options? To obey human reason? Or to downsize and work within our means and watch God's resources flourish?

In the end, added funds would have caused us to continue the status quo instead of working through the hard choices. After months of prayer, counsel, and deliberation, we made the brutal decision to end our bicycle division in April 2014. Downsizing and ending something is never easy, especially when it means saying goodbye to faithful volunteers and the success that helped us reach this point in our ministry. However, it also freed us to concentrate on what we did best, our hand-pedaled trike.

By then we had distributed more than 1,700 bicycles and donated the rest of the inventory to another bicycle organization. This made it possible to move our trike division into a 250-square foot Public Storage unit for under $200 a month. The climate-controlled lighted space guaranteed that our raw steel parts wouldn't rust.

Two months later, we hosted a meeting at the storage unit with a representative from a mobility company that by then had distributed nearly one million wheelchairs to people in almost one hundred countries. They initiated the meeting after reviewing our free online downloadable trike plans as they began to explore adding a hand-pedaled trike to their product line. It confirmed that we had accomplished our goals: a space that held our inventory, decreased our overhead, and still allowed us to display our ministry.

At the time of HWI's transitional stage, from fall 2013 to summer 2014, my church's life was in a bleak season. I wondered, *How can I serve in a way that facilitates healing and not further division within the congregation?* God used three verses of Scripture to pique my curiosity and to provide my next prayer assignment. "And there was a prophetess, Anna the daughter of Phanuel, of the tribe of Asher. She was advanced in years and had lived with her husband seven years after her marriage, and then as a widow to the age of eighty-four. She never left the temple, serving night and day with fastings and prayers. At that very moment she came up and began giving thanks to God, and continued to speak of Him to all those who were looking for the redemption of Jerusalem."[211]

Anna intrigued me, and I found myself wanting to know more of her story than the eighty-four words Luke writes. After obtaining permission and receiving a room key to the church's nursing station, I was set. I now had my "Anna Prayer Closet" where I could spend extended periods of two to three hours at a time. There, over a seven-month period, I began discovering answers to my questions about Anna: *What did she do all that time in the temple? Didn't it get boring? What kept her there?*

Within a few days, I came to understand that it would have taken volumes to capture all that happened through Anna's dedication to praying—the ultimate Masada snake-path prayer adventure. I also got a glimpse of how she was center stage to all the action.

As for me, here are some of the things I did and discovered during my "Anna prayer time."

I began by instituting three things: be still, be present, and keep my eyes open to what was going on around me. Having begun during the gorgeous fall season, I spent an hour in each of seven different locations around the perimeter of the church. On one occasion I prayer-walked, picking up garbage as I circled the property. Some observations I made were that the cracks and faded blacktop made the parking lot look run down; the playground equipment was dilapidated; and the front entrance lacked curbside appeal. Then, what a prayer thrill to hear during an annual church meeting two years later that the church had budgeted for new playground equipment. In addition, I knew God heard my prayers when I noticed that the church had spruced up the front entrance and that the parking lot had a fresh coat of blacktop.

On a bright Saturday, I arrived midmorning to a deserted church parking lot. I trembled at the thought of sitting on the front porch, facing Roosevelt Road, a major artery, guitar in hand, worshipping the name of Jesus. *I don't want to look stupid. Will the police come by and run me off? What will I say if someone asks what I'm doing here?* Across the road, I spotted a woman gardening in front of her house. *Would such thoughts ever cross her mind?* Not once did she glance over at me, leaving me to wonder, *What's her history with our church?*

I remember the first time I knelt in my "Anna Prayer Closet." It was overwhelming, as sixty years of church history rushed into my prayers. I wrote, "The walls cried out with the prayers from saints of old who had trod these halls and were now part of the great cloud of witnesses. Chills went down my spine, as I thought of the choir, complete with these promoted members singing in the heavenly Temple. The opening and closing creaks of the doors declared that a constant flow of people still come in daily, even though all reports made it sound like the church was on life support."

On another occasion, I brought my burdened request to the Lord as I wrote,

"Prayer is the only answer for the depth of despair in our culture today. Yet Satan has neutralized it at best or, more accurately, created such mass confusion and division over even the Word and its activity. It has left Christian leaders asking, "Could you define what you mean by prayer?"

During my "Anna Prayer Closet" season, a nearby church had a continuous 24/7 prayer time in their chapel for one hundred days, culminating on April 20, 2014, Easter Sunday. What an amazing opportunity to spend time there too. One day I saw a child praying alongside his mother, heard another whispering to the Lord, and watched someone else enter. What a delight to see prayer modeled—caught, not just taught, to children. It was a beautiful picture of multigenerational opportunity where a ten-, twenty-, thirty-, fifty-, and seventy-year-old were gathered—when sixty days earlier there were only two. It inspired me to pray, "Lord, may prayer become a deeply-rooted place in the spiritual lives of churches and Christians within DuPage County. May there be a twenty-four-hour space always open—a prayer shelter."

One morning after a friend had spent the night at my home, I wanted to show her something unique in the area and thus decided to take her to the Prayer Chapel. There we crashed a prayer party. It happened soon after settling in, as the church's fourteen-member worship team entered. They said, "We have reserved this hour, but you are welcome to stay."

The singing left me thinking, *There's nowhere I'd rather be*, as I was serenaded by the harmonizing group. All our sniffles and tears were part of the Holy Spirit's cleansing delight. As our prayers went up as incense, it was a glimpse of heaven on earth. While taking it all in, my friend mouthed, "WOW!" and later said, "It doesn't get any better than this." Prayer hospitality was something I'd never experienced before and it left me longing for more!

On another day at the same Prayer Chapel, I crashed a clergy's time slot. After spending some spontaneous time praying together, I told him about Pray 10K. He encouraged me to write the book and offered to read the chapters and give input along the way. He began with, "Ask a group of people to pray for you as you write the book. I'd be honored to be a Pray 10K prayer partner." God used this divine appointment as an answer to a prayer I had written thirteen years earlier: "If my prayer life is to be put in book form, show me when and how to do it." Then eighteen months after beginning to write Pray 10K he e-mailed me, "I am preaching about prayer . . . May I draw on some of your insights?"

My Anna Prayer Closet season ended so I could begin the next assignment, writing the book. Below are some of the other outgrowths and insights that came from that time.

One weeklong activity I did during our summer Backyard Bible Club (BYBC) was to pray on location. The Monday morning I was to begin, June 17, 2014, I awoke at 4:30 a.m., feeling anxious. Fretting, I wondered, *Will I be sneered at by the other volunteers for just praying while they are busy working with the children? Did Anna ever feel sneered at or mocked?* My fears proved unfounded, but Satan hoped to deter me from participating.

It was prohibitive for me to roam around outside where the programs were taking place, given that the temperatures were in the upper nineties. Instead, for three hours a day I prayed, sitting in an air-conditioned family room overlooking the flurry of activity through the huge picture window.

One evening the daughters at the host house asked, "Mom, what is she doing sitting inside while BYBC is going on outside?" When the mother explained that I was praying, she later told me it sparked quite the dialogue as she answered her daughters' questions, "What could someone pray about for three hours?" God used my actions as a prayer mentor to these young girls, an answer magnanimously larger than I could have ever imagined.

Another outgrowth occurred in 2015, when I prayed at our church's Vacation Bible School (VBS). The theme for the week compared our spiritual life to that of Mount Everest. At the beginning of the week, the leader made an announcement: "Children, let me introduce you to Miss Teisan. You will see her throughout the week. She is praying for VBS and each of us. If you want her to pray for you, she'd be happy to do so. Feel free to talk with her. Or you can just stop by and see the picture she is drawing while praying today."

Each day, I did a different pencil drawing prayer. These included pictures designed with words in the form of a lake, a mountain, a tree planted by the water, and a bowl with prayers going up as incense. Some days the prayers were complete sentences, other days they were just a word in the form of a leaf. As I moved along with the children to different stations, they would come and inquire, "What's the prayer picture of the day?" By incorporating pencils, drawing, and words, I was modeling a way they could replicate this prayer form at home, showing them that prayer can be a creative, fun, and practical way to connect with God.

The curiosity from the children was my opening for a private teachable prayer moment. I'd ask, "Do you have anything you'd like me to pray about?" After the child shared, I continued, "Could I pray with you right now?" Once they agreed, we paused amid the activities and together conversed with the Lord. By doing so, it let them know God cares about their personal concerns, and that we as leaders do too.

Then on the last day, I had each child write his or her name in my prayer sketchpad. By doing so, I conveyed to each of them that they were special in God's eyes and that I would pray for them. I was amazed at the unique way each child expressed themselves by the choice of color, style, size, and placement of their name. It was a prayer closure for the week.

Participating in such a way with VBS showed me how important it is to include a prayer component alongside the programming side, where we model the importance of prayer to children, parents, and leaders.

The more time I spent in my "Anna Prayer Closet," the more I began to see what fascinated Anna and kept her attention. God transformed my heart, renewing a passion within for the church.

I also began noticing all the people in Scripture where we just get a tidbit of information. They're teasers, as the "movie trailers" for the story God wants to write through our journeys. When we give ourselves to be a character in the Gospel message, we no longer have a need to vicariously live through another, or to say, "I'm so jealous: I envy what you have or are able to do."

Personal Prayer: Heavenly Bridegroom, I want to thank you for cherishing your bride, the church. Forgive me, for I don't always have the same love for her as you do. Forgive me for the times I want to be anywhere but doing what you've called me to do—PRAY! May I always remember that communion with you is a gift. I pray that you'd continue your refining work even more. I long for an uninterrupted intimacy with my Savior. Thank you, Lord Jesus, for the discernment you give through prayer. Amen.

QUESTIONS:
1. How would you define prayer?
2. Share an onsite prayer experience you've had or one that you may try.
3. Share a time when God answered your prayer through another person.

Epilogue

Debriefing

The only touch which reaches God is that of faith. The multitude may throng and press; but heart to heart, soul to soul, mind to mind only so do we come in actual contact with God.
—Fredrick William Robertson

PRAYER IS A BASIC essential of the spiritual life, a barometer indicating the state of my soul. When I'm intentionally developing and deepening my relationship with Christ, I find myself running less at the mouth with people and running more often to God. When I'm in a rattled, rushed, ragged, and restless rut, my time log reveals the root cause—a lack of refreshment and renewal with my Redeemer.

I have gained an ever-broadening understanding of what it means to "pray without ceasing."[212] When the light bulb went on, I began to understand how my thoughts are prayers: *Wow what a warm day. Aren't the clouds beautiful? I enjoyed a crisp walk today.* Remarks are also prayers, "Being with you today was such a joy. Thank you!"

Wonders, too, are worship as I marvel at the buds on a tree in early spring, a reminder of the Resurrection—that out of death comes new life.

Through practicing spiritual ear training, hearing the Lord's still, small promptings, I've responded more often to the premonitions and his whispers, such as, "Oh, you should call the store before going to see if they are open. Don't go today. Wait until tomorrow. E-mail that friend right now and tell them you are praying for their situation." In addition, when I face insomnia in the wee hours of the morning, I've used those times for prayer. If a specific person or event comes to mind, I pray, knowing this is God's guiding, too. When disability causes me to cancel plans, I've begun to approach it with a prayerful wonder, *What's on his agenda instead?*

Early on, I'd force myself to stay on track—*concentrate, Alice, concentrate!* But, why wouldn't I daydream? It's part of the DNA God designed within me, a visionary. Who better to share these musings with than the "Ultimate Dream Weaver"?

One tool I've implemented when stuck is going from A to Z as an acrostic, the format of Lamentations and many psalms. For example, "Lord, thank you for A, apples, B, buds on trees, C, Colors you created, D, daylight, . . . T, Teisans, U, unity . . . Y, your love, Z , zeal for life. Worship and lament are the major grease components that lube my prayer chain.

The Lord has allowed me to travel farther around the world and accomplish more while physically incapacitated in my "main office" than I ever did before prayer was my number one occupation.

I leave you with one warning. Satan tries to do whatever he can to prevent us from discovering the intimacy of communing with the Lord described in Scripture. "O taste and see that the Lord is good; how blessed is the man who takes refuge in Him!"[213] Because once we've experienced intimacy with Christ, it creates an insatiable hunger for more—and there's no turning back. Paul wrote, "I count all things to be loss in view of the surpassing value of knowing Christ

Jesus my Lord, for whom I have suffered the loss of all things, and count them but rubbish so that I may gain Christ."[214]

On September 2, 1998, only four months into my prayer journey, I had scribbled down many of my questions. Two of them were, *What would a prayer occupation look like? How would I know when prayer had become my number one occupation?* Doubts raged! I feared prayer was a polite way for God to say, "Alice, you're benched, red-carded, out of the game for good!" *Will I have to wait until I get to heaven to know if my prayer life made a difference?* Being a frail human, I certainly hoped not! I needed a few encouragements along the way to silence my fears and to see that prayer was placing me in a leadership position equal to a team captain.

In April 2016, David Cox wrote the following about ME/CFS in *The Guardian*, "Yet for much of the past three decades, CFS has been treated as the proverbial skeleton in the closet of the medical world. Potential researchers have been scared off by the stigma associated with the disease, and government funding has been nonexistent. 'When I was a medical student in the 90s, we were instructed that CFS patients could not be seen in our clinic,' Montoya recalls. 'And a letter was sent out to those patients telling them not to come.'"[215] Through prayer, God has transformed my stigmatized disability into a leadership asset. The severe limitations have provided the latitude needed for embracing divine interruptions and the Holy Spirit's nudgings.

Now, more than 4,000 hours into my second Pray 10K, I am grateful I made prayer my number one occupation. I'm beginning to understand that "praying without ceasing" is a lifestyle that requires bringing every aspect of life into sync with the Lord's plan. A way of "joining in helping us through your prayers, so that thanks may be given by many persons on our behalf for the favor bestowed on us through *the prayers of* many."[216] As I heard people's feedback, I realized anew the richness of this verse. The verse gives me hope that God has created me with a soul capacity to pray in such a way, but it will require continued discovery on my part.

Twenty-six years after I questioned my occupation, in 2014, a Wheaton College Graduate scholar from Africa asked, "What is the one task you spend the most time on in your position as executive director of His Wheels International?" Having just calculated my prayer time for the last twelve months, I answered, "Prayer! I prayed three and a half hours a day last year, 1,277 hours." Afterward I thought, *WOW—prayer has become my number one occupation!* Moreover, indeed my number one responsibility with HWI is to lead from a posture of prayer, as Jesus modeled.

That same fall, I told the story of both HWI and Pray 10K during a college chapel. The next day while meeting with several student groups, I received similar questions from many of them. "How do you begin an organization? How do you pray an hour a day?" I recounted this to a faculty member, and he said, "Millennials are hungry and are wondering how to develop a relationship with the living, all-powerful God! We all need your story."

In 2015, when reminiscing at HWI's ten-year annual Board meeting, Harv, who refers to himself as a Jewish Atheist, said, "The highlight for me is the opening and closing prayer at every Board meeting. Each one is unique and from the heart!"

The same year, while meeting with another HWI friend, he said, "I don't know if I've ever told you this, but years ago, our church was in a desperate place. I had no idea what we were to do. Because of your example, I instituted a church prayer hour once a week. You'd never believe what is happening as the result of prayer." *What?* I couldn't believe this was the same guy who back in 2010, when I told him prayer was our fund-raising method, said, "Yes, but God gave you a brain and he expects you to use it."

God also highlighted an unexplainable component of prayer. He fulfilled a secret lifetime desire—an impossible one (or so I thought!)—*to have been born a few hundred years earlier so I could have invented something helpful for society.* It had been a prayer! The Eternal Innovator had placed an unfathomable desire for innovation within me!

The first confirmation had come on January 12, 2012, through an e-mail that was forwarded to me. It was from the cofounder of a cycling company that began in 1997. Their production focused on specialty bikes for the disabled, with an emphasis on serving those in Africa. He had written, "Thank you for the His Wheels info. Their DOTT [Dual Offset Tube Trike] hand-trike is one of the best. Their note on fitting is in accordance with much of what we have learned in the last decade of building adaptive bikes, trikes and quadracycles." The affirmation about the high quality of our trike was confirmed after the director of a leading recumbent company attended an ergonomics seminar the HWI team presented. Both compliments demonstrated yet again that God knows my dreams before I ask and that he alone can bring them to fruition.

Another area in which the Lord prompts is on domestic issues. For instance, five days after my friends moved into a new home, having had many days of heavy rains, I e-mailed them. "Praying for you—that homeownership hasn't proven to put you underwater! How did you weather the storm?" Twenty minutes later, I received a response. "Wow, AT. I've always known you had a straight line to God. We had a foot of water in the basement tonight . . . Thanks for the prayers—we needed (need!) them. ☺"

I wrote back, "Sorry to hear about the water, will keep my line to God open." She replied, "Seriously, AT, it was such an encouragement to get your message at the very moment we needed it." They had just written an e-mail seeking professional counsel about the situation and she wrote, "We had just hit the send button—literally one minute later (in the time it took to send the message), your e-mail popped up. It felt like a reminder from God that he was with us and he had prompted you to pray. Amazing . . . Thank you for the good storm—the storming of heaven!—in the midst of our other storm!"

The next year while at a healthcare appointment there was someone shadowing the clinician. The observer said, "Your joyful spirit is infectious." *Wow!* Those words were as valuable as gold. Matthew Henry writes, "Prayer is heart's ease to a gracious soul."[217]

On another occasion in 2016, I went to an Ethiopian restaurant for lunch with two friends, Grace and Carolyn. It's always a fun experience since Carolyn, a blonde Caucasian, has spent at least three decades in Ethiopia as a missionary and speaks Amharic. During our visit, Carolyn and the owner engaged in conversation, an invitation for the owner to talk about her homeland. She said, "I always pray for my country," while looking at Grace, the oldest of us, who compassionately listened, having spent seven years as a missionary in Uganda.

As they talked, God challenged me, "Offer to pray for Ethiopia now." My heart sank. *Now? Lord? Really, are you sure?* I confessed to feeling self-conscious and afraid of rejection. After a small protest, I asked, "Could we pray for your people right now?" Immediately she pulled out a chair at the table, sat down, and reached out her hands for us all to join hands as she said, "Oh yes. Thank you." I prayed for the people of Ethiopia, Uganda, and Zimbabwe, the African countries where the three of us had done mission work. It was also a moment of prayer evangelism, and an invitation for her to continue talking. When we finished, I gave the owner a copy of my story, complete with the story of salvation, in a three-fold 750-word professionally printed tract. Writing the tract was a challenge my friend Bob Walker gave me back in 2009.

As 2016 was ending, I received the following e-mail from David, a medical doctor and HWI friend, "I am traveling to Timbuktu, Mali, on December 28 with a medical mission. I don't know for sure if they could use a trike, but would that be a possibility? . . . It would be cool if you could add Timbuktu to your map!" What David didn't know is back in 2011, when reading a missionary's story about his time in Timbuktu, I thought, *Wow! I'd love to send a trike there one day.*

Once I confirmed David could take a trike, he checked with his contact in Mali who said, "We already know about HWI and have even tried to build the trike here." As I look back I wonder, *Had my desire to send a trike to Timbuktu been a thought or a prayer?* Only the Lord could orchestrate such a divine encounter and answer such an extravagant prayer in his way and his time.

The ultimate affirmation I received was the one reminding me that I am still a sinner, in need of continuing with a spirit of humility and an attitude of reverence while growing in my relationship with Christ. A reminder of Paul's words, "Therefore let him who thinks he stands take heed that he does not fall."[218]

After removing the boots that I had used while turning my compost pile, I decided to put them in "a safe, clean spot," the recycle bin, to air out. As I was doing so, I began debating with the Lord's whisper of reason that went like this, "Don't do it; you will forget, and they will be mistakenly thrown out." I don't know why I picked a debate with the Lord, but I did! I rationalized his advice away, *No, I won't forget. I don't want to put them in the garage for the spiders and other critters to make a new home. Nor do I want to leave them outside in case it rains. And I certainly don't want to take these smelly boots into the house.*

The Lord was merciful and gave me a second opportunity to obey the night I took out the trash. This time the still small voice of reason said, "Don't take it out tonight. It's raining, you're tired, and the container isn't full. Wait until next week." By then I would have needed the boots again. For now, all I can do is hope my new winter boots will be a reminder to listen and obey, and not debate God's leading!

My ludicrous debate reminds me of Job's debate with God, and God's reprimand: "Who gives intuition to the heart and instinct to the mind? . . . Do you still want to argue with the Almighty? You are God's critic, but do you have the answers?"[219] I'm left to ponder and respond to these same questions. And how about you?

Thus, I continue my Masada snake-path prayer ascent knowing that the Masada cable-car prayer ascent is worthless. David Thomas writes, "No one can carry thee up the 'holy hill' of true greatness. Thou must climb its height thyself—thou must weave thine own crown—rear thine own throne. The 'Father hath prepared' them for thee, but they must be wrought out of, and by the powers He has given thee."[220]

Only after I finished writing this book did I learn from Harvey that he took his bike on the Masada cable car. At the age of 61, in 1988, carrying it up the path was more than he could do. I asked him, "Why didn't I do that too?" He said, "You wouldn't hear of such an option. To you the trip wasn't complete unless you along with the other young people went up struggling, carrying your bike up the Masada Snake Path." I don't remember this, but Harvey reminded me, "You said, 'if I'm going to get up there, I'm going to do it the way the Jews did it back then—and it wasn't by cable car.'" I want to model my prayers after the example of Jesus' communion with his Abba Father—taking all the necessary time, with the same urgency, and not looking for shortcuts.

I could never have imagined how HWI would provide a platform whereby I could share my life of suffering, prayer, faith, hope, and transformation with individuals from many tribes, tongues, and nations, without it requiring a passport for travel.

For example, there's no way I could have ever anticipated the remark I'd receive in 2016 while talking with Tom Rickert, the founder and executive director of Access Exchange International (AEI). For more than twenty-five years, AEI, a not-for-profit and nongovernmental agency, has continued to "promote inclusive public transport for persons with disabilities in Africa, Asia, the Americas, and eastern Europe. [AEI assists] stakeholders in less-wealthy regions as they promote, plan, and implement inclusive bus, rail, and paratransit services for seniors and passengers with disabilities."[221]

Tom said, "Your HWI vision for trikes fits perfectly within the 2015–2030 United Nations Sustainable Development Goals. Both 10.2 and 11.2 target inclusion and access by persons with disabilities and other vulnerable groups. 10.2 states 'By 2030, empower and promote the social, economic and political inclusion of all, irrespective of age, sex, disability, race, ethnicity, origin, religion or economic or other status.'[222] And 11.2 states 'By 2030, provide access to safe, affordable, accessible and sustainable transport systems for all, improving road safety, notably by expanding public transport, with special attention to the needs of those in vulnerable situations, women, children, persons with disabilities and older persons.'[223] It is obvious that this is what you are doing."

Man-made entertainment, including extreme sports thrillers, pale in comparison to the holy extravagant adventures I would have missed if I hadn't embarked on the most rigorous, demanding, extreme Pray 10K challenge. How about you? What blessings would God like to shower on you through prayer? Is he encouraging you to take a radical prayer step?

Regardless of the place in which I find myself each day, transcending all my circumstances and limitations, the occupation of prayer continues to provide me with the thrill of soaring on the wings of eagles, the adventure of traveling to the ends of the earth, and the deepening in my intimacy with the King of Kings, my Abba Father. As I continue growing, the words of Isaiah sink ever deeper into my soul: "But there the majestic One, the LORD, will be for us a place of rivers and wide canals on which no boat with oars will go, and on which no mighty ship will pass."[224] My health condition is limiting, allowing me to manage only a mustard seed amount of activity, but through prayer God has multiplied my efforts and allowed my life to flourish as an oak of righteousness.

Commissioning Prayer: As this travelogue concludes, I pray the words of Paul for each of us as we continue our unapologetic journey of faith: "I ask—ask the God of our Master, Jesus Christ, the God of glory—to make you intelligent and discerning in knowing Him personally, your eyes focused and clear, so that you can see exactly what it is He is calling you to do, grasp the immensity of this glorious way of life he has for His followers, oh, the utter extravagance of His work in us who trust Him—endless energy, boundless strength!"[225] I end with this blessing of Paul, "To Him be the glory in the church and in Christ Jesus to all generations forever and ever. Amen."[226]

QUESTIONS:
1. What have you learned from reading Pray 10K?
2. What do you hope to implement into your prayer life?
3. How has the book encouraged you?
4. What reminds you to listen and obey?

Appendix

The Lord's Prayer
A Concert of Prayer

The Model Prayer: Matthew 6:9-13

RACING THROUGH THE LORD'S Prayer in the "rote-memory-mode" was effortless, but when I tried reciting it in a contemplative manner, it was incomprehensible. In search of discovering the scope covered in four verses, I prepared a compilation of quotes and Scripture verses. I use it as a guide during my personal time and in a large group context as a concert of prayer. The goal is not to make it through all the material at once, but to have some new and stimulating ideas about each phrase.

This tool can be beneficial for individual, private prayer, or for group and corporate prayer settings. Moreover, it is intended to prompt your intercessions on behalf of family, church, work, missions, government (local, state, national, and international), the world, etc.

> *Our Father in heaven, hallowed be your name. Your kingdom come, your will be done, on earth as it is in heaven. Give us this day our daily bread, and forgive us our debts, as we also have forgiven our debtors. And lead us not into temptation, but deliver us from evil: For thine is the kingdom, and the power, and the glory, for ever. Amen.*
> —Matthew 6:9-13, *New International Version*

Our Father in heaven, Reveal who you are. Set the world right; Do what's best—as above, so below. Keep us alive with three square meals. Keep us forgiven with you and forgiving others. Keep us safe from ourselves and the Devil. You're in charge! You can do anything you want! You're ablaze in beauty! Yes. Yes. Yes.
　　　　　　　—Matthew 6:9-13, *The Message*

"Our Father in heaven" (Matthew 6:9)

- "Whatever ideas of immensity, grandeur, unsearchableness, spirituality, purity, blessedness, perfection, the dome of heaven suggests—all this, and infinitely more, we are to ascribe to Deity, when we lift up our hearts in prayer."[227]

Thus says the Lord: 'Heaven is my throne, and the earth is my footstool; what is the house that you would build for me, and what is the place of my rest?'
—Isaiah 66:1

For you did not receive the spirit of slavery to fall back into fear, but you have received the Spirit of adoption as sons, by whom we cry, 'Abba! Father!' The Spirit himself bears witness with our spirit that we are children of God.
—Romans 8:15-16

But the hour is coming, and is now here, when the true worshipers will worship the Father in spirit and truth, for the Father is seeking such people to worship him.
—John.4:23

Additional: John 16:23; 20:17; Galatians 4:6; Ephesians 4:6; 1 John 3:1

"Hallowed be your name" (Matthew 6:9)

- Its first three petitions are for God and his glory. . . . May his name be treated reverently and may all that is about him—his Word and his gospel—be regarded with the deepest awe![228]

Blessed be the name of the LORD *from this time forth and forevermore! From the rising of the sun to its setting, the name of the* LORD *is to be praised!*
—Psalm 113:2-3

For from the rising of the sun to its setting my name will be great among the nations, and in every place incense will be offered to my name, and a pure offering.
—Malachi 1:11

To you I lift up my eyes, O you who are enthroned in the heavens!
—Psalm 123:1

Additional: 1 Chronicles 16:28-30; Ezekiel 36:23; Psalm 77:11-15; Isaiah 6:1-8; Revelation 7:9-12

"Your Kingdom Come" (Matthew 6:10)

- "It is therefore perfectly legitimate for us to use the petition with our minds specially directed toward the consummation of Christ's reign, the complete establishment of his Kingdom, his final glorious triumph, when the kingship (sovereignty) of the world, shall become our Lord's and his Christ's."[229]

And the kingdom and the dominion and the greatness of the kingdoms under the whole heaven shall be given to the people of the saints of the Most High; their kingdom shall be an everlasting kingdom, and all dominions shall serve and obey them.
—Daniel 7:27

Ask of me, and I will make the nations your heritage, and the ends of the earth your possession.
—Psalm 2:8

Then I heard what seemed to be the voice of a great multitude, like the roar of many waters and like the sound of mighty peals of thunder, crying out, "Hallelujah! For the Lord our God the Almighty reigns.
—Revelations 20:6

Additional: Matthew 7:21; Revelations 11:15; 12:10; 1 Chronicles 16:31-34

"Your will be done on earth as it is in heaven" (Matthew 6:10)

- "We desire for the supreme will to be done in earth, with a cheerful, constant, universal obedience like that of heaven. . . . Our heart's highest wish is for God's honor, dominion and glory."[230]

Do not be conformed to this world, but be transformed by the renewal of your mind, that by testing you may discern what is the will of God, what is good and acceptable and perfect.
—Roman 12:2

For this is the will of God, your sanctification: that you abstain from sexual immorality.
—I Thessalonians 4:3

And so, from the day we heard, we have not ceased to pray for you, asking that you may be filled with the knowledge of his will in all spiritual wisdom and understanding.
—Colossians 1:9

Additional: Psalm 103:20-21; Matthew 12:50; Ephesians 6:6; I Thessalonians 5:18; Hebrews 10:36; 13:21; 1 Peter 2:15; 4:2

"Give us this day our daily bread" (Matthew 6:11)

- "My friend, every time a loaf of bread appears on your table, it really is as much the result of a miracle as was the manna which fell in Arabia, or the cruse of oil which failed not the widow of Zarephath," (I Kings 17:8-24) or the five loaves and two small fishes which fed famishing thousands. . . . Our Heavenly Father would have us modest in our requests. . . .

He would have us ask Him only for bread, type of whatever is really needful for our well-being."[231]

But if we have food and clothing, with these we will be content.
—I Timothy 6:8

Remove far from me falsehood and lying; give me neither poverty nor riches; feed me with the food that is needful for me, lest I be full and deny you and say, 'Who is the LORD?' or lest I be poor and steal and profane the name of my God.
—Proverbs 30:8-9

The young lions suffer want and hunger; but those who seek the LORD lack no good thing.
—Psalm 34:10

Additional: Job 23:12; Matthew 7:7; John 4:34; Isaiah 55:1-5

"Forgive us our debts, as we also have forgiven our debtors" (Matthew 6:12)

- "'The life sustained by daily bread is not enough; we need also the forgiveness of sin'" (Weiss).[232]

I have blotted out your transgressions like a cloud and your sins like mist; return to me, for I have redeemed you.
—Isaiah 44:22

If you, O LORD, should mark iniquities, O Lord, who could stand? But with you there is forgiveness, that you may be feared.
—Psalm 130:3-4

My little children, I am writing these things to you so that you may not sin. But if anyone does sin, we have an advocate with the Father, Jesus Christ the righteous. He is the propitiation for our sins, and not for ours only but also for the sins of the whole world.
—1 John 2:1-2

Additional: Psalm 51; 103:8-12; Isaiah 31:1; 55:7, Jeremiah 31:34; Micah 7:18–19; Matthew 18:21-22; Luke 6:37; Acts 13:38; Ephesians 1:7; 1 John 1:9

"Lead us not into temptation. But deliver us from evil" (Matthew 6:13)

- "All life is a ceaseless temptation: that is to say, a ceaseless testing, probing; or, to use a familiar but profound phrase, Life is a Probation. . . . The probe which our Father means for our advantage Satan may turn to our disadvantage."[233]

Watch and pray that you may not enter into temptation. The spirit indeed is willing, but the flesh is weak.
—Matthew 26:41

No temptation has overtaken you that is not common to man. God is faithful, and he will not let you be tempted beyond your ability, but with the temptation he will also provide the way of escape, that you may be able to endure it.
—1 Corinthians 10:13

The LORD will keep you from all evil; he will keep your life.
—Psalm 121:7

Additional: 1 Chronicles 4:10; Luke 22:31-32, 46; John 17:15; Romans 3:10, 2 Thessalonians 3:3; 2 Timothy 4:18; 2 Peter 2:9; Revelation 2:10

"For thine is the kingdom, and the power, and the glory, for ever. Amen." (Matthew 6:13)

- "That devotion which begins with prayer ends in praise. All rule, and might, and honor, belong to God; and to him let them for ever be ascribed. His is the 'the kingdom', or the right to rule; 'the power', or the might to uphold his authority; and 'the glory', or the honor that comes out of his government."[234]

Yours, O Lord, is the greatness and the power and the glory and the victory and the majesty, indeed everything that is in the heavens and the earth; Yours is the dominion, O Lord, and You exalt Yourself as head over all. Both riches and honor come from You, and You rule over all, and in Your hand is power and might; and it lies in Your hand to make great and to strengthen everyone. Now therefore, our God, we thank You, and praise Your glorious name.
—1 Chronicles 29:11-13

But as for me, I will hope continually, and will praise You yet more and more.
—Psalm 71:14

Additional: Psalm 41:13; 72:18-20; 150

Acknowledgments

WHERE DO I BEGIN? Even though my name appears on the cover, my entire network has contributed to seeing this project from a concept to a finished manuscript. There are the cheerleaders, editors, artists, prayer partners, endorsers, coaches, teachers, readers, and those who've walked each step of this journey with me. Just listing a few of the categories makes me tremble as I think of the names that fit within each category. I am forever grateful for your sacrifice of time and your unique gifts and talents that helped make my dream a reality. "To the only God our Savior, through Jesus Christ our Lord, be glory, majesty, dominion and authority, before all time and now and forever. Amen."[235]

I'd cherish receiving a note, a picture, a prayer, or a memory from new and old friends as a reminder of just how many have had a part in HWI and or my Pray 10K journey.

Alice Teisan
His Wheels International
PO Box 423
Wheaton, IL 60187
www.hiswheels.org
info@hiswheels.org

209

Notes

Introduction
[1]Deuteronomy 4:29, NASB
[2]1 Timothy 3:16, AMPC
[3]1 Corinthians 2:7, 9-10
[4]Joseph A. Seiss, *Gospel In Leviticus* (Kregel Publications, Grand Rapids, MI: 1981, original printing 1860), 119–20.

Chapter 1
[5]I John 1:9, NASB
[6]I Timothy 2:5, NASB
[7]Kroll, *Bible Country*, 105–7.
[8]Sandi Patty, *Via Dolorosa* (Nashville, TN: Word/Curb/Warner, 2008).
[9]Mark 14:32-37, ESV
[10]Psalm 121:1-2, ESV
[11]Alice Teisan, *Riding on Faith: Keeping Your Balance When the Wheels Fall Off* (Wheaton, IL, 2012). Content in chapter 1 has been adapted from portions of chapter 2 (11–12), 4 (31).
[12]Alexander Maclaren, *Expositions of Holy Scripture*, vol. 4 (Grand Rapids, MI: Eerdmans, 1944), 336.
[13]Ibid., 339.
[14]John Gill, An Exposition of the Old Testament: In Which the Sense of the Sacred Text Is Taken, vol. 3 (London: William Hill Collingridge, 1851, 1960), 359.
[15]Maclaren, Expositions of Holy Scripture, 340–41.
[16]Ibid., 342.

Chapter 2
[17]Matthew 26:40, NLT

[18] Kroll, *Bible Country*, 72.

[19]Teisan, *Riding on Faith*. Content in chapter 2 has been adapted from portions of chapter 4 (31), chapter 5 (40–41), and chapter 2 (12–14).

[20]Psalm 18:2, NASB

[21]John A. Broadus, *An American Commentary on the New Testament, Gospel of Matthew* (Valley Forge, PA: Judson Press, 1886), 131.

[22]Luke 11:1, NASB

[23]Ibid., personalized

[24]George Dana Broadman, *Studies in the Mountain Instruction* (New York: Appleton and Company, 1901), 248.

Chapter 3

[25]"How Great Thou Art," EMI CMG Publishing, 1953, http://www.hymns.me.uk/how-great-thou-art-hymn.htm

[26]Ibid.

[27]Ibid.

Chapter 4

[28]See http://www.businessballs.com/erik_erikson_psychosocial_theory.htm

[29]Deuteronomy 23:23, NASB

[30]See "Freedom to Pray," http://calvinquotes.com/tag/prayer/

[31]1 Samuel 3:5, NASB

[32]1 Samuel 3:10-11, NASB

[33]Psalm 141:2, NASB

Chapter 5

[34]Matthew 6:6, ESV

[35]Kroll, *Bible Country*, 109.

[36]Ibid

[37]NLT *Chronological Life Application Study Bible* Footnote (Carol Stream, IL:Tyndale, 2012), 431.

[38]1 Corinthians 6:19-20, NASB

[39]"Essential Tourist Information for Visiting Masada," accessed 3/23/16, http://masadatours.com/essential-tourist-information-for-visiting-masada

[40]Philippians 3:10, ESV

⁴¹Ibid.

⁴²Broadus, American Commentary on the New Testament, 130.

⁴³Ibid.

⁴⁴Maclaren, Expositions of Holy Scripture, 236.

Chapter 6

⁴⁵2 Corinthians 3:18, NASB

⁴⁶Ephesians 1:3-4, NASB

⁴⁷2 Peter 3:9, NASB

⁴⁸Romans 8:26, ESV

⁴⁹Richard Box, Denis John-Naylor, Carole Massey, Sally Michel, and Ronald Swanwick, *Drawing Step-by-Step* (Great Britain: Search Press Limited, 2009), 12.

⁵⁰See https://www.goodreads.com/author/quotes/30510.John_Calvin

⁵¹See http://vangoghletters.org/vg/letters/let549/letter.html

⁵²"List of 10 Remarkable Religious Renaissance Paintings" *History Lists,* http://historylists.org/art/list-of-10-remarkable-religious-renaissance-paintings.html

⁵³See *Khan Academy,* https://www.khanacademy.org/humanities/renaissance-reformation/renaissance-venice/late-renaissance-venice/a/transcript-of-the-trial-of-veronese

⁵⁴Ibid.

⁵⁵*The Sonnets of Michelangelo Buonarroti,* trans. S. Elizabeth Hall (London: Kegan Paul, Trench, Trubner & Co., Ltd.), 148.

⁵⁶Eugene H. Peterson, *Under the Unpredictable Plant* (Grand Rapids, MI: Eerdmans, 1992), 101.

⁵⁷Ibid.

⁵⁸Ecclesiastes 1:9, ESV

⁵⁹William Gurnall, *A Treatise of the Whole Armor of God, Part 1* (1657), 4–5. https://www.ccel.org/ccel/gurnall/armour/files/armour1.pdf

⁶⁰Stuart Hample and Eric Marshall, *Children's Letters to God* (New York: Workman Publishing Company, 1991).

⁶¹Matthew Henry, *New One Volume Edition Commentary on the Whole Bible* (Grand Rapids, MI: Zondervan, 1977), 1512.

⁶²Galatians 5:1, NASB

Chapter 7
[63]Ephesians 6:12, NASB
[64]*Calvin: Institutes of the Christian Religion*, ed. John T. McNeill, trans. Ford Lewis Battles (London: Westminster John Knox Press, 1960), 850.
[65]Galatians 5:1, NASB
[66]Arthur W. Pink, *The Ability of God* (Chicago, IL: Moody Publishers, 2000), 58.
[67]Ephesians 6:10-11, NASB
[68]Ephesians 6:13-17, NASB
[69]See http://www.moodyradio.org/chris-fabry-live; Teisan, *Riding on Faith*. Content in chapter 7 has been adapted from portions of chapter 15 (185–86).
[70]Ephesians 6:19-20, NASB
[71]Psalm 27:8, NLT

Chapter 8
[72]Psalm 139:23-24, NASB
[73]Ephesian 4:26, NASB
[74]Evelyn Christenson, *What Happens When Women Pray* (Wheaton, IL: Victor Books, A Division of Scripture Press Publications, Inc. 1975).
[75]John 8:32, ESV
[76]James 1:20-21, NASB
[77]Psalm 139:15-16, NASB

Chapter 9
[78]1 Samuel 8:22, NASB
[79]Gill, Exposition of the Old Testament, 141.
[80]Jeremiah 1:6-7, NASB
[81]Psalm 108:13, ESV

Chapter 10
[82]Teisan, *Riding on Faith*. Content in chapter 10 has been adapted from portions of chapter 1 (5) and chapter 4 (30–31).
[83]Joshua 4:5-7, ESV
[84]Jennifer Martin, "The 7 Psychological Stages of Chronic Pain," *Pain News Network*,

http://www.painnewsnetwork.org/stories/2015/9/13/the-7-psychological-stages-of-chronic-pain-illness

[85]See "Leaving Frailty Behind," http://med.stanford.edu/news/all-news/one-to-one/2016/a-conversation-with-laura-hillenbrand.html, (4 min. mark).

[86]ME/CFS is known by other names.

[87] Katrina Berne, *Chronic Fatigue Syndrome, Fibromyalgia and Other Invisible Illnesses* (Amanda, CA: Hunter House Inc., 2002), 24.

[88] See http://consults.blogs.nytimes.com/2009/10/15/readers-ask-a-virus-linked-to-chronic-fatigue-syndrome/

[89]Anne Ortegren, "From International Traveler to 43 Square Meters: An ME/CFS Story From Sweden," *Health Rising*, March 28, 2014, https://www.healthrising.org/blog/2014/03/28/from-international-traveller-mecfs-report-stay-home-prison-can-anyone-hear/

[90]See "The Blue Ribbon Foundation Medical Fellowship" video, http://www.eaglerarelife.com/content/ryan-prior, (0–30 sec. marker).

[91]Henry, New One Volume Edition Commentary on the Whole Bible, 1442.

[92]Arthur T. Pierson, *George Muller of Bristol and His Witness to a Prayer-hearing God* (New York: Fleming H. Revell Company, 1919), 15.

Chapter 11

[93]See http://remote.health.vic.gov.au/viccdb/view.asp?Query_Number=2075

[94]David Tuller, "How 'Chronic Fatigue Syndrome' Obscures A Serious Illness," *BuzzFeed*, January 27, 2014, http://www.buzzfeed.com/davidtuller/chronic-fatigue-syndrome

[95]Exodus 4:2-4, NASB

[96]Ibid.

[97]See "*The Karate Kid* Quotes," *Internet Movie Database*, 2010, http://www.imdb.com/title/tt1155076/quotes

[98]1 Samuel 15:22, NASB

[99]Philippians 4:19, NASB

[100]Hebrews 4:12, NASB

Chapter 12

[101]Thomas, Gospel of Matthew, 548.

[102]D. Baldwin, MD, endocrinologist at Rush St. Luke's Medical Center Hospital

[103]Teisan, *Riding on Faith*. Content in chapter 12 has been adapted from portions of chapter 5 (41–42) and chapter 7 (75).

[104]Evan Howard, "*Lectio Divina* in the Evangelical Traditions," *Journal of Spiritual Formation & Soul Care*, vol. 5, No. 1 (2012): 56–77.

[105]Ibid., 58.

[106]Richard J. Foster, *Prayer: Finding The Heart's True Home* (San Francisco, CA: Harper, A Division of Harper Collins Publishers, 1994), 256.

[107]David H. Stern, *Jewish New Testament* (Jerusalem, Israel: Jewish New Testament Publications, 1989), 98.

[108]Howard, "*Lectio Divina* in the Evangelical Traditions," 56–77.

[109]Ibid., 65, quoting Lewis Bayly, *The Practice of Piety*, 51st ed. (London: Daniel Midwinter, 1714), 140.

[110]Howard, "*Lectio Divina* in the Evangelical Traditions," 68.

[111]Proverbs 15:22, ESV

Chapter 13

[112]Lynn Vanderzalm, Finding Strength in Weakness: Help and Hope for Families Battling Chronic Fatigue Syndrome (Grand Rapids, MI: Zondervan, 1995), 215.

[113]Colossians 1:16-17, NASB

[114]Psalm 98:1, NASB

[115]Robert Alter, *The Book of Psalms* (New York: W.W. Norton & Company, 2007), 345.

[116]Ibid.

[117]Sandra D. Wilson, Into Abba's Arms: Finding the Acceptance You've Always Wanted (Carol Stream, IL: Tyndale, 1998) 33.

[118]Psalm 116:5, 7, NASB

[119]See #35 in http://prayer-coach.com/2010/08/23/prayer-quotes-andrew-murray/

[120]Ibid., #33

[121]Henry, New One Volume Edition Commentary on the Whole Bible, 286.

[122]Luke 11:24-26, NASB

[123]Colossians 3:2, NASB

[124]Maclaren, Expositions of Holy Scripture, 226-27.

[125]Ibid., 228.

[126]Robert Alter, *The Book of Psalms* (New York: W.W. Norton & Company, 2007) 221.

[127]Acts 20:35, NASB

[128]Luke 12:48, NASB

[129]Thomas, Gospel of Matthew, 70.

[130]Acts 17:28, NASB

[131]Henry, New One Volume Edition Commentary on the Whole Bible, 642.

Chapter 14

[132]Teisan, *Riding on Faith*. Content in chapter 14 has been adapted from portions of chapter 6 (60-61).

[133]Jeremiah 1:4-8, AMP

[134]Matthew 19:19, NASB

[135]Romans 8:28, NASB

[136]Luke 12:48, NASB

[137]John. 8:32, NASB

[138]Psalm 18:19, NIV

Chapter 15

[139]Genesis 9:6, NASB

[140]Gill, Exposition of the Old Testament, 141.

[141]1 Corinthians 6:19

[142]Vidhima Shetty, "Former Cal Student Struck by Disease," *The Californian*, September 29, 2016, http://www.thecalifornianpaper.com/2016/09/former-cal-student-struck-by-disease/?utm_content=buffer8f8e0&utm_medium=social&utm_source=facebook.com&utm_campaign=buffer

[143]See "The Blue Ribbon Foundation Medical Fellowship" video, http://www.eaglerarelife.com/content/ryan-prior, (45–50 sec.).

[144]Ibid., (55–60 sec.)

[145]Ibid., (1.29–1.32 min.)

[146]Proverbs 18:14, NASB

[147]Isaiah 41:10, NIV

[148]Psalm 31:15, NASB

[149]Proverbs 16:3, NASB

[150]Romans 5:1, NLT

[151]Teisan, *Riding on Faith*. Content in chapter 15 has been adapted from portions of chapter 5 (48–49).

[152]Henry, New One Volume Edition Commentary on the Whole Bible, 282.

[153]"Awesome Beauty" (Daphne Rademaker), Vineyard Music Discography

[154]Ibid.

[155]Henry, New One Volume Edition Commentary on the Whole Bible, 283.

Chapter 16

[156]Jeremiah 17:7-8, NLT

[157]Teisan, *Riding on Faith*. Content in chapter 16 has been adapted from portions of chapter 6 (56–60, 69–70), chapter 7 (71, 76–78), and chapter 8 (97–98).

[158]C. H. Spurgeon, *The Treasury of the Old Testament*, vol. 4 (London: Hunt, Barnard & Co., Ltd., 1934), 451.

[159]Hebrews 13:2, NASB

[160]Psalm 18:33, NLT

Chapter 17

[161]Teisan, *Riding on Faith*. Content in chapter 17 has been adapted from portions of chapter 8 (101–105) and chapter 11 (133–34).

[162]1 Samuel 9:15-16, NASB

[163]Henry, New One Volume Edition Commentary on the Whole Bible, 294.

[164]Ibid.

[165]1 Samuel 7:12, NASB

Chapter 18

[166]Elizabeth Goudge, *My God and My All: The Life of Francis of Assisi* (New York: Coward-McCann, 1959), 48.

[167]1 Peter 3:15, ESV

[168]Teisan, *Riding on Faith*. Content in chapter 18 has been adapted from portions of chapter 13 (155–56).

169Priscilla Shirer, *Discovering the Voice of God: How to Recognize when God Speaks* (Nashville, TN: Lifeway Press, 2008), 111.
170Isaiah 56:7, NASB
171Haggai 2:7, 9, NASB
172Ephesians 1:17, NASB
173Oswald Chambers, *My Utmost for His Highest* (New York: Dodd, Mead & Company, 1935), 89.
174David McCasland, *Oswald Chambers Abandoned by God* (Grand Rapids, MI: Discovery House, 1993), 42.
1751 Corinthians 7:32-35, NASB
176See http://www.mcheyne.info/calendar.pdf
177Andrew Hess, "What to Say When You Pray," *Boundless* (blog), May 9, 2013, http://www.boundless.org/blog/what-to-say-when-you-pray (quote by Robert Murray M'Cheyne)
178See http://www.mcheyne.info/calendar.pdf

Chapter 19
179Joshua 1:9, AMP
1802 Corinthians 12:9, NASB
181Luke 22:42, NASB
1821 Chronicles 29:11-12, ESV
183Spurgeon, Treasury of the Old Testament, 499.
184Jeremiah 29:13, ESV
185Psalm 66:5, NIV

Chapter 20
186See http://www.boblosteamers.com/ (Bob-Lo Steamer Ship Specs 1902–1991)
187Daniel 6:10, NASB
188C. H. Spurgeon, "Commenting on Commentaries, Lecture 1: A Chat About Commentaries (1834-1892)," *The Spurgeon Archive*, 2001. http://www.spurgeon.org/misc/c&c.php
189Henry, "Revelation, The Crossway Classic Commentaries," in *Matthew Series Editors Alister* (Wheaton, IL: Crossway Books, 1999), ix.
190Judge 6:16, NASB
191Henry, New One Volume Edition Commentary on the Whole Bible, 249.
192Maclaren, Expositions of Holy Scripture, 220–21.

[193]Ephesians 6:11, NASB
[194]Thomas, Gospel of Matthew, 10.
[195]See http://stanmed.stanford.edu/2016summer/leaving-frailty-behind.html
[196]Matthew 24:4-8, NASB

Chapter 21
[197]Isaiah 12:5-6, KJV
[198]Henry, New One Volume Edition Commentary on the Whole Bible, 846.
[199]John 15:5, NASB
[200]See http://library.timelesstruths.org/music/It_Is_Well_with_My_Soul/

Chapter 22
[201]Henry, New One Volume Edition Commentary on the Whole Bible, 1832.
[202]Psalm 31:5, NASB
[203]Broadus, American Commentary on the New Testament, 53.
[204]Matthew 7:7-8, NASB
[205]Thomas, *Gospel of Matthew*, 75.
[206]Henry, New One Volume Edition Commentary on the Whole Bible, 610.
[207]1 Timothy 2:1-2, NASB
[208]Jason Mandryk, *Operation World*, 7th Edition (Downers Grove, IL: IVP Books, an imprint of InterVarsity Press, 2011).
[209]Ibid., xviii.
[210]Ecclesiastes 7:1-4, NASB

Chapter 23
[211]Luke 2:36-37, NASB

Chapter 24
[212]1 Thessalonians 5:17, NASB
[213]Psalm 34:8, NASB
[214]Philippians 3:8, NASB
[215]David Cox, "Is Chronic Fatigue Syndrome Finally Being Taken Seriously?" *The Guardian*, accessed December 10, 2016,

https://www.theguardian.com/lifeandstyle/2016/apr/04/chronic-fatigue-syndrome-cfs-taken-seriously

[216]2 Corinthians 1:11, NASB

[217]Henry, New One Volume Edition Commentary on the Whole Bible, 282.

[218]1 Corinthians 10:12, NASB

[219]Job 38:36; 40:2, NLT

[220]Thomas, Gospel of Matthew, 395.

[221]See http://www.globalride-sf.org/about.html

[222]See https://sustainabledevelopment.un.org/sdg10

[223]See https://sustainabledevelopment.un.org/sdg11

[224]Isaiah 33:21, NASB

[225]Ephesians 1:15-19, MSG

[226]Philippians 3:21, NASB

Appendix A

[227]George Dana Broadman, *Studies in the Mountain Instruction* (New York: Appleton and Company, 1901), 230-31.

[228]C. H. Spurgeon, *The Gospel of the Kingdom, A commentary on the book of Matthew*, (Pasadena, TX: Pilgrim Publications, 1893, reprint 1996), 34.

[229]Broadus, American Commentary on the New Testament, 134.

[230]C. H. Spurgeon, The Gospel of the Kingdom, 34.

[231]Broadman, Studies in the Mountain Instruction, 237.

[232]Broadus, American Commentary on the New Testament, 137.

[233]Broadman, Studies in the Mountain Instruction, 241–42.

[234]C. H. Spurgeon. The Gospel of the Kingdom, 35.

Acknowledgements

[235]Jude 1:25, NASB

Made in the USA
Columbia, SC
11 November 2018